iPhone 12

The Illustrated Step by Step Guide with Tips and Tricks to Master the New iPhone 12, Mini, Pro, and Pro Max

Abraham Bentley

Table of Content

Introduction

Apple released four iPhone models in 2020: the iPhone 12 Mini, iPhone 12, iPhone 12 Pro, and iPhone 12 Pro Max, all at different prices and screen sizes. The iPhones have the new A14 processor, new MagSafe charging system, 5G connectivity, and new camera/ video features. The major differences between each model are the camera features and size.

The iPhone 12 is available in five colors at a base price of $799. The 12 Mini begins at $699, 12 Pro at $999, & the 12 Pro Max at $1,099. The iPhone 12 Pro Max was released on November 13 alongside the iPhone 12 Mini, while the iPhone 12 and iPhone 12 Pro shipped on October 23.

The iPhones have several new features, better cameras, new colors, new designs, and a better processor. The iPhones have OLED Super Retina XDR screen displays, with the non-Pro models having lower-quality displays. The iPhone 12 and 12 Mini are considered the non-pro models, while the iPhone 12 Pro and 12 Pro Max are considered the Pro models.

The iPhone 12 Mini is the smallest with its 5.4-inch screen size, the iPhone 12 has a screen size of 6.1-inch, iPhone 12 Pro has a 6.1-inch screen size, and the iPhone 12 Pro Max has a 6.7-inch screen display.

The iPhone 12 Pro and 12 Pro Max have a triple-camera system and LIDAR on the back of the device, while the iPhone 12 and 12 Mini has a dual-camera system. The Pro models of the iPhone 12 have the ProRAW feature, a new imaging format that combines computational and RAW photography features like Smart HDR and Deep Fusion to give the photographer full control over the dynamic range, details, and color on the Camera app. The iPhone 12 Pro and iPhone 12 Pro Max also have the new LiDAR sensor that uses time-of-flight calculations to show a 3D map of your environment.

Inside the back of all the iPhone 12 models is a circular arrangement of magnets that makes it possible for users to use the MagSafe for wirelessly charging your iPhone 12. Asides from using it to charge your device, you can also use the built-in magnet to attach accessories, sleeves, cases, and wallets to your iPhone.

The four iPhone 12 models are the first iPhone to have the A14 Bionic chip upgrade, which improves the devices' efficiency and speed. The A14 Bionic chip offers 40% more transistors than the version before it, offering faster performance and better battery life.

The iPhone 12 models are also the first iPhone to support 5G networks on both the Sub-6GHz 5G and the mmWave. mmWave 5G networks are known to be the fastest 5G speed available in the tech space today. However, the mmWave is short-range and can be interrupted by trees, buildings, and obstacles. This is where the Sub-6GHz 5G covers up – this 5G network is more widespread and available in different regions in the United States and other countries, including suburban, rural, and urban areas. 5G offers improved FaceTime call quality, faster uploads and download speed, and increased bandwidth for live streaming. Note that the 5G network drains your battery faster than 4G and should be turned off when not needed.

Chapter 1: Setting Up Your iPhone 12

Follow the steps below to power on and set up your iPhone on your first use:

- Press down the Side Button until the screen lights up, and the Apple logo shows on your screen, then select your language and country.

- Click on **Set Up Manually** and continue with the steps presented on your screen. This step is for persons who do not own any other Apple device. If you have another Apple device (iPad, iPod Touch, or a different iPhone), you may use the **QuickStart** option to automatically move your settings and data from the Apple device to your iPhone 12. If this applies to you, place the two Apple devices beside each other, then follow the steps presented on your screen to copy files from one Apple device to the iPhone 12 and complete the setup.

Hello

Quick Start

Bring your current iPhone or iPad near this
iPhone to sign in and set up.

If your other iPhone or iPad doesn't show
options for setting up this iPhone, make
sure it's running iOS 11 or later, and has
Bluetooth turned on. You can also set up
this iPhone manually.

Set Up Manually

Copy Data to your iPhone 12 from an Android Device

Asides from moving data from another Apple device, you can also copy content from an Android device to your iPhone 12 when setting up your device the first time or after erasing your iPhone.

- Connect to Wi-Fi on the iPhone and Android, then plug the two devices into a power source.

- Download the '**Move to iOS**' app on your Android device.

- Press down the Side Button on your iPhone 12 until the screen lights up.

- Continue with the steps presented on your screen until you see the **Apps & Data** screen.

- Select **Move Data from Android** and launch the **Move to iOS** app on the Android device. Tap **Continue,** read the terms of service, then click **Agree.**

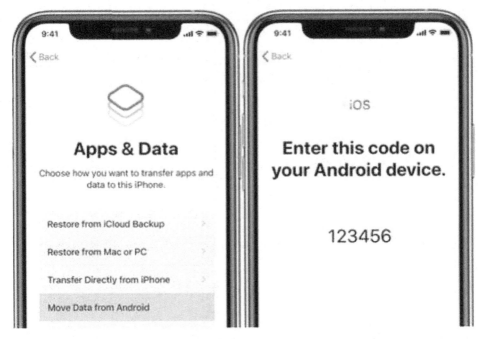

- Still on the Android device, tap **Next,** then tap **Continue** on the screen of the iPhone 12.

- A code will pop-up on your iPhone screen; input the code on the displayed field on your Android device.

- Choose all the items you want to copy, then tap **Next.** After the device is done moving your content, tap **Continue** on your iPhone and tap **Done** on your Android device.

- Then continue with the steps presented on your screen to set up your iPhone 12 completely.

Sign in with Apple ID

You need the Apple ID to access services like iMessage, iCloud, FaceTime, Books, etc. While you can operate your Apple device without having an Apple ID, you should create one to enjoy exclusive services from Apple. For the Apple ID, you will need to provide your email address and password. The service will also store your security details, contacts, and payment methods you use across all the Apple services you access.

The first time you power on your phone, you will see the prompt to sign in to Apple ID. You will also receive the option of doing this at a later time. If you already have an Apple ID account, use the steps below to sign in on your iPhone 12:

- Open the Settings app and tap the **'Sign in to your iPhone'** option at the top of your screen.
- Input your Apple ID and its password.
- You may be prompted to enter a 6-digit code that will be sent to your phone number or your trusted device to finish signing in.

Create an Apple ID

Follow the steps below to create an Apple ID for new users:

- Open the iOS app store and click on your profile image.
- Tap the **'Create New Apple ID'** option and enter your desired email address and password.

- Then select a region or country that is the same as the billing address on your payment cards.

- Go through the terms of service, click on **Agree to Terms and Conditions,** then tap **Next.**

- Put your name and birthday in the right fields, then press to subscribe to Apple Updates if you desire.

- Input your card details, then tap **Next** or tap **None** to proceed without inputting this information.

- Check that your phone number is correct, then tap **Next.**

- Apple will then send a verification email to your registered email address. Follow the instructions in the email to verify your email address on Apple ID.

Set up and Customize your iCloud Settings

The first time you power on your iPhone 12 and begin the setup process, you will see the prompt to store your data on iCloud Drive. If you declined the service at the point of set up, you could follow the steps below to set up and customize your iCloud settings manually.

- Click on your name in the **Settings** app and tap **iCloud.**
- Then toggle on the apps you wish to use with the iCloud Drive, like Calendar, Contacts, and third-party applications.

Set Up eSIM on iPhone 12

Apple allows users to use both a physical SIM and an eSIM on the iPhone 12. An eSIM, like the name implies, is stored digitally on the iPhone. You can choose to set up cellular service on your iPhone 12 using the eSIM alongside the physical SIM. To set up,

- Click on **Cellular** in the **Settings** app and tap **Add Cellular Plan.**

- Using your device camera, capture the QR code that your carrier provided. You may also enter the details manually.

- Then tap **Add Cellular Plan** to finish. If you choose to use the eSIM as your second line, you will receive further prompts to change some settings.

Switch Between eSIMs

You can set up more than one eSIM on your device, but you cannot use more than one eSIM at a go. To move between eSIMs,

- Click on **Cellular** in the **Settings** app.

- Click on the plan you want to switch to, then tap the '**Turn on This Line**' option.

Wake iPhone

- Raise your iPhone or tap the screen to wake the iPhone 12.

The 'Raise to Wake' feature is enabled by default. To disable it,

- Tap **Display & Brightness** in the **Settings** app, then turn off the '**Raise to Wake**' switch.

Rename your Device

The name of your device is what shows when sharing hotspots and the likes. To rename the device,

- Click **General** in the **Settings** app, tap **About,** and tap the '**Name**' option.

- Tap the icon, enter a name, and tap **Done.**

Customize Sound and Vibration

Choose sounds to work with different features on your device.

- Click on **Sounds & Haptics** in the **Settings** app, then scroll to **Ringers and Alerts** and use the slider underneath it to modify the volume for all system sounds.

- To customize vibration and tones for different sounds, tap a sound type, then swipe through the tones until you get to the one you like.

Set Up Dark Mode

Dark mode makes it easy to use your iPhone in a low-light environment. To turn on Dark Mode,

- Tap **Display & Brightness** in the **Settings** app, then click the 'Dark' option to turn on **Dark Mode.**

- Turn on the '**Automatic**' switch if you want Dark Mode to come on automatically at a specific time.

- Then click on **Options** to create a Dark Mode schedule of your choice.

Automatically Adjust Screen Brightness

Customize your screen brightness to adjust automatically using the lighting condition of your current environment.

- Tap **Accessibility** in the **Settings** app.
- Click **Display & Text Size**, then turn on the **'Auto-Brightness'** switch.

Set Device Time and Date

- Tap **General** in the **Settings** app, then click on **Date & Time.**
- Choose the **'Set Automatically'** option if you want the date and time to change automatically depending on the time and date in your current location. Disable this option if you want to enter the time and date manually.
- The **'24-Hour Time'** option will display the hours on your device using the 0 to 23 hours format rather than the 1 to 12 hours format

Turn on Night Shift

This feature uses the time on your device to know when it's sunset in your area and then automatically changes your screen colors to warmer colors. The device switches back to its regular settings in the morning. To turn this feature on automatically,

- Tap **Display & Brightness** in the **Settings** app, then click the **'Night Shift'** option to turn it on.
- Move the switch beside **Scheduled** to the right, then scroll to **Color Temperature** and use the slider to control the color balance for the Night Shift.
- Tap **From** and choose an option from the drop-down list.

Power Off Your Device

There are two ways to power off your iPhone.

- Tap **General** in the **Settings** app, click **Shut Down,** and then use the **Power Off** slider to turn off your device.

- Press the Side button and any of the Volume buttons to bring up the **Power Off** slider, then pull the slider to the right to turn off your device.

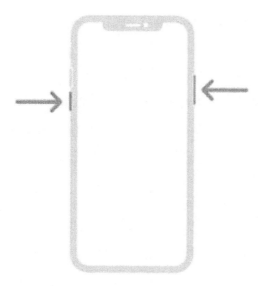

Power On Your Device

- Continue to press the side button until your screen lights up.

Force Restart an iPhone

This setting takes care of hanging apps and unresponsive screen.

- Press the volume up button quickly and release it immediately.

- Press the volume down button quickly and release it immediately.

- Now press firmly on the side button until your screen lights up.

Chapter 2: Basic Settings

Change the Wallpaper

- Tap **Wallpaper** in the Settings app and select the **'Choose a New Wallpaper'** option. Then do any of the following:

➢ You may choose to use a preset image at the top of your screen. The images that have the ◐ mark changes when you turn on **Dark Mode**.

➢ Choose from your personal photos: click an album and touch the image you want to use.

➢ Tap the ⬒ button to switch on the **'Perspective Zoom'** (this feature is limited to certain wallpaper choices). This setting makes it seem as if your wallpaper is moving when you rotate your device.

- After you have selected your wallpaper preference, tap **Set,** and choose an option from the pop-up: **Set Home Screen,**

➢ **Set Lock Screen** or **Set Both**

You can also switch on the Perspective Zoom option for your existing wallpaper. To do this,

- Tap **Wallpaper** in the Settings app, click the image on your Home or Lock Screen, then click on **Perspective Zoom.**

Use a Live Photo as Wallpaper

Live Photos can be used as a wallpaper on the Lock screen - after you set up the wallpaper, tap and hold the Lock Screen to play the Live Photo video.

- Tap **Wallpaper** in the Settings app and select the '**Choose a New Wallpaper**' option.
- Click on '**Live**' and then choose the Live Photo you want. Or, click on the Live Photo album to select a Live Photo.
- Tap '**Set**' and click on **Set Lock Screen.**

Access Features from the Lock Screen

While your screen is locked, you can open the Control center, view your notifications, open the camera, and more. From the Lock screen,

- Swipe left to open the camera.
- Swipe up from the center of the lock screen to view your notifications.
- Swipe up from the bottom end of your screen to open the Control Center.
- Swipe right on the Lock screen to see **Today View.**

Control Access to Info on the Lock Screen

Choose the features that you can access on the iPhone lock screen.

- Tap **Face ID & Passcode** in the Settings app, then switch on the options you want.

Show Notification Previews on the Lock Screen

Notification Previews include details about your calendar invitations, lines from emails received, and text from your received messages.

- Tap **Notifications** in the Settings app.
- Tap the '**Show Previews**' option and then click on **Always.**

Chapter 3: Notifications on iPhone 12

The Notification tab gives you recent updates of events on your device like missed calls, new messages, and more. You can customize the notification settings to show you only what you wish to see.

View Your Notifications

As notifications come into your device, you can click on it to view it right away. But if you do not read the notifications as they come, you can go to the Notification Center to see all you missed. You can go to the notification center in any of the ways below:

- Swipe down from the topmost center part of your screen to display the notification center. Or swipe up from the middle of the lock screen to display the notification center when your device is locked.

- To expand group notifications, click the group notification, and you will see the different notifications under the group. Click the **'Show Less'** option to close the group notification.

- Press a notification to view the app that owns the notification.

- Press and hold the notification to read it or perform quick actions available on the app.

- Use one finger to swipe up from the bottom of your screen to close the Notification center.

Manage Notifications

- If a notification comes in while using another app, you can pull down the notification to see it, then swipe up to dismiss the notification.

- If you receive a notification and do not want to view it immediately, you can send it to the Notification Center – swipe left over the notification(s), click **Manage,** then tap the '**Deliver Quietly'** option. This will stop notifications from that app from popping up on the Lock Screen, showing a banner, lighting up your screen, or playing a sound. If you want to allow notification from that app in the future, go to the Notification Center, swipe left over a notification from that app, tap **Manage,** then click the '**Deliver Prominently'** option.

- To clear or dismiss notifications, swipe left on the notification(s), then click the '**Clear'** or '**Clear All'** option.

- To mute notifications for a group or an app, swipe left over the notification(s), tap **Manage** and then click the "**Turn Off"** option.

- To delete all the notifications in the Notification Center, tap and then click the '**Clear'** option.

- To customize how you want to see notifications from an app, swipe left on the notification from that app, tap **Manage,** click on **Settings,** then select an option like whether to play an alert sound, where to show the notifications, and more.

Change Notification Settings

The iPhone allows you to customize Notification settings for individual apps. You can change the alert sound, choose where the notifications should appear, set up location-based alerts, and more.

- Tap **Notifications** in the Settings app and then customize your options.

- To customize when the notification previews should appear, click the '**Show Previews'** option and then choose an option – **When Unlocked, Always** or **Never.**

- Use the Back button to go to the previous screen, scroll to **Notification Style,** and tap an app, then turn the '**Allow Notifications'** switch on or off. If you turned on the switch, select where and how the app's notifications should appear: in Notification Center or on the Lock Screen.

- Tap the '**Notification Grouping'** option and then select how you want your device to group the notifications:

  - ➤ Select the '**By App'** option to group together all notifications from one app.

  - ➤ Select the '**Automatic'** option to group the notifications by the existing criteria within the app.

  - ➤ Tap the '**Off'** option to disable grouping.

Selectively Turn Off Notifications for Apps

To disable notifications for individual apps,

- Tap **Notifications** in the Settings app.

- Click on '**Siri Suggestions'** and turn off the notification for each app.

Show New Notifications on the Lock Screen

To access the Notification Center while your device is locked,

- Click **Face ID & Passcode** in the **Settings** app and enter your passcode.
- Scroll to the **'Allow Access When Locked'** section and turn on the **'Notification Center'** switch.

Silence All Notifications

To mute all notifications,

- Click **Do Not Disturb** in the Settings app and then turn on the **'Do Not Disturb'** switch.

Set Up Location-Based Alerts

Some apps on your iPhone send you alerts that may be relevant to you based on your location. For instance, you may receive a notification to text someone when you arrive at a location. You can turn off these alerts if you do not like them.

- Tap **Privacy** in the Settings app and click on **Location Services.**
- Turn on the **'Location Services'** switch.
- Then click an app and choose to either share your location when using the app or not.

Get Government Alerts

Certain regions or countries have Government Alerts like the Emergency, Public Safety, and AMBER alerts for users in the United States or the Emergency Earthquake Alerts for users in Japan. To turn on these alerts on your iPhone,

- Click **Notifications** in the Settings app, then move to the **'Government Alerts'** screen and turn on the switch for the options you want.

Chapter 4: Do Not Disturb

Do Not Disturb (DND) is a quick way to mute your iPhone. It mutes incoming calls & notifications. It also stops your screen from lighting up.

Turn on Do Not Disturb

- Swipe down from the upper right part of your screen to go to the control center, then tap the 🌙 button turn on Do Not Disturb. The 🌙 icon will show on the status bar to alert you that DND is on.

- To set an end time for DND, press the 🌙 button in the Control Center until you see a pop-up, then choose the time you want. You may also tap the **'Schedule'** button at the bottom of the pop-up, turn on the **'Scheduled'** switch, and then choose the start and end times.

Allow Calls when DND is On

DND ensures that incoming calls are muted. But you can allow your device to ring out for select calls.

- Tap **Do Not Disturb** in the Settings app.

- Then tap the '**Allow Calls From**' option to allow calls from selected contacts.

- Turn on the '**Repeated Calls**' switch to allow your phone to ring out when a number calls you repeatedly.

Allow Calls From Emergency Contacts when DND is On

Set up people that can reach you when you turn on DND

- Open the Contacts app, click on a contact and tap **Edit.**

- Click the '**Ringtone or Text Tone**' option and then turn on the '**Emergency Bypass**' switch.

Schedule Quiet Hours

Set up the times that you do not want any notifications or disturbances on your device.

- Tap **Do Not Disturb** in the Settings app.

- Turn on the **Scheduled** switch and then choose the start and end time for your quiet hours.

Customize Do Not Disturb Settings

You can configure the DND settings to silence the iPhone only when your device is locked or unlocked.

- Tap **Do Not Disturb** in the Settings app.

- Tap the **'Always'** option to silence your device whenever you turn on DND.

- Tap the **'While iPhone is Locked'** option to silence the device only when you lock your device.

Turn on DND while Driving

Turn on the **Do Not Disturb While Driving** option to limit or silence text messages and other notifications while driving. To receive calls, you need to connect your device to your car's Bluetooth or the CarPlay. Siri can also help you read your messages if you request.

If you did not turn on **Do Not Disturb While Driving** and the iPhone detects you may be driving, it will send you a notification to turn it on. See how to turn on the option manually.

- Tap **Do Not Disturb** in the Settings app.

- Tap **Activate** close to the end of your screen.

- Then choose an option for turning on the **Do Not Disturb While Driving** option.

  - Tap **Automatically** to permit your device to turn on the feature once it detects you may be driving.

  - Tap **Manually** to turn it on yourself in the Control Center.

  - Tap the **'Activate with CarPlay'** option to instruct the DND option to come on once you connect your device to CarPlay.

  - Tap the **'When Connected to Car Bluetooth'** option to automatically turn it on when your device is connected to your car's Bluetooth system.

Add Do Not Disturb While Driving to Control Center

To manually control the **Do Not Disturb While Driving** option, you will need to visit the control center. To add the feature to the Control Center,

- Tap **Control Center** in the Settings app, then tap the  button beside the '**Do Not Disturb While Driving'** option

Get Notifications when You are a Passenger

If you are being driven, you can turn off the **Do Not Disturb While Driving** feature.

- Press the '**Do Not Disturb While Driving'** reminder on your lock screen and then click '**I'm Not Driving.'**

- Or swipe up from the end of your screen and press the **I'm not Driving** option.

Send Automated Text Messages when Driving

With **Do Not Disturb while Driving** active, anyone in your Favorite group who messages you will receive an auto-reply informing them that you are driving. To change the recipients of these auto-replies,

- Tap **Do Not Disturb** in the Settings app.
- Click on **Auto-Reply To** and choose an option:
  - ➢ Tap **No One** to stop sending auto-replies.
  - ➢ Tap **Recents** to send to people that contacted you within the last two days regardless of if you saved their numbers.
  - ➢ Tap **Favorites** to send to anyone in your Favorite group.
  - ➢ Tap **All Contacts** to send to everyone in your Contacts.
- If the person replies with the word **'Urgent,'** all the other texts from that person will be allowed for the rest of the drive.

Create Custom Auto-Reply Text Message

To create your own auto-reply messages,

- Tap **Do Not Disturb** in the Settings app.
- Click on **Auto-Reply To** and click a default message, then write your preferred message.

Allow Some Calls

If your vehicle does not have CarPlay support or Bluetooth, you can permit some calls to come in while you are driving.

- Tap **Do Not Disturb** in the Settings app.
- Click on **Allow Calls From** and choose the contacts you want.

To allow a second call from someone within three minutes,

- Tap **Do Not Disturb** in the Settings app and turn on the **Repeated Calls** switch.

Chapter 5: Family Sharing

Members of a family sharing group can share their screen time information, subscriptions, purchases, and lots more. The group is created by a member of the family, who then adds up to five other family members to the group. Each iPhone user can only belong to one family group per time.

Set Up Family Sharing

- Tap your name in the **Settings** app, tap **'Family Sharing.'**
- Tap **Set Up Your Family** & continue with the steps presented on your screen to create the family sharing group & add members.

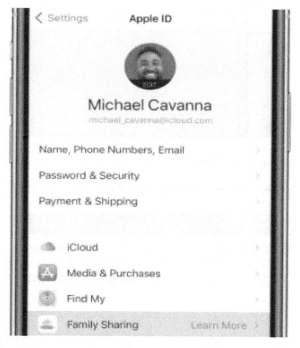

Add a Family Member

After creating a family sharing group, the organizer can add more members to the group with the steps below:

- Tap your name in the **Settings** app, then select **Family Sharing.**
- Click on **Add Member,** click on **Invite People,** then continue with the steps presented on your screen to complete.

Disable Family Sharing

The group organizer can close the family sharing group whenever he or she wishes.

- Tap your name in the **Settings** app, then select **Family Sharing.**
- Click on your name again, and tap the '**Stop Using Family Sharing**' option to exit the group without closing it or tap the '**Stop Using Family**' option to remove every member of the group and close the group.

Remove Someone from the Family Group

This can only be done by the person that created the group.

- Tap your name in the **Settings** app, then select **Family Sharing.**

- Tap the person you want to delete, then tap the **'Remove (Name) From Family'** option.

Download Family Members' Purchases

Members of a family sharing group can choose to share their purchases with other members of the same group.

Download Shared iTunes Store Purchases

- Launch the iTunes store on your device, tap **More,** and tap the **'Purchased'** option.

- Choose the family member that made the purchase and choose a category.

- Click on the item you want to download and tap ⬇️ .

Download Shared iOS App Store Purchases

- Launch the App store on your device, tap your profile image, and then tap the **'Purchased'** option.

- Choose the family member that made the purchase and tap by the side of the desired item.

Stop Sharing Purchases with Family Members

Group members can disable purchase sharing if they choose not to share their purchases with the rest of the family group.

- Tap your name in the **Settings** app, then click **Family Sharing**.

- Press **Purchase Sharing** and now turn off the **'Share Purchases with Family'** switch.

- The group founder can also choose to stop sharing his purchases with others – simply tap **'Stop Purchase Sharing.'**

Enable Ask to Buy for Children

Turn on this option if you want all the purchases made by children in the group to be authorized by the group founder, guardian, or parent.

- Tap your name in the **Settings** app, then click **Family Sharing**.

- Press **'Ask to Buy,'** select the child, and turn on the **'Ask to Buy'** switch.

Share iCloud Storage and Subscriptions with Group Members

Share your iCloud storage and various subscriptions with your family members.

- Tap your name in the **Settings** app, then tap the **'Family Sharing'** option.

- Select the subscription you want to share and continue with the steps presented on your device.

Share Your Location with Family Members

When setting up the group, the group founder will receive a prompt to share his location. If he accepts, the group founder's location will be available to all members of the group. The rest of the group can also choose to share their location to easily locate missing devices and view each other's location in the Find My app.

The first step is to turn on **Location Services,**

- Tap **Privacy** in the **Settings** app, then turn on the '**Location Services'** switch.

Then continue with the guide below:

- Tap your name in the **Settings** app, and select **Family Sharing.**
- Click on **Location Sharing** and turn on the '**Share My Location'** option.
- If you aren't already sharing your location, you should select the '**Use this iPhone as my Location'** option on your screen.
- Choose the people that can view your location, then select '**Share My Location.'** You will need to choose a family member per time until you have selected all the family members you want.
- If you do not want one of the group members to continue accessing your location, click on the person and tap the '**Stop Sharing my Location'** option.

Chapter 6: Update, Reset and Restore

Let us look at some of the settings that you will often need on your device.

Update Device Automatically

Turn on this option if you want the Apple device to update automatically whenever a new software is available.

- Tap **General** in the **Settings** app and select **Software Update.**

- Tap **Customize Automatic Updates** and then toggle on your desired options on the next screen.

Update Device Manually

If you do not sign up for the Automatic update, you can search for and manually install software updates on your iPhone.

- Tap **General** in the **Settings** app and select **Software Update.**

- Any new update will show on this screen. Click on an update to download and install it.

Backup Device using iCloud

Backup your iPhone content on iCloud Drive.

- Click your name in the **Settings** app, tap **iCloud,** and then tap the 'iCloud Backup' option.

- Move the switch beside **'iCloud Backup'** to the right to turn it on.

- iCloud will automatically run a daily backup when your phone is locked, connected to power, and on Wi-Fi.

View iCloud Backups

To see all the items you backed up on iCloud Drive,

- Click your name in the **Settings** app, and tap **iCloud.**

- Click on **Manage Storage** and tap the **'Backups'** option to see all the backups.

- To discard a backup, tap the backup and press **Delete Backup.**

Restore Device Settings to their Default

Restore the different settings on your device to their default. You need to back up your device before you perform any of these actions.

- Tap **General** in the **Settings** app, press the **'Reset'** option, then choose the appropriate option on your screen:

- ✓ Tap **'Reset All Settings'** to return all the settings on your device to their default without losing your media or data.

- ✓ Click **Reset Network Settings** to wipe off all changes you made to the network settings.

- ✓ Click on **Reset Home Screen Layout** to wipe off every saved change you made on the home screen layout.

- ✓ Click on **Reset Keyboard Dictionary** to wipe off all the words you added to the default dictionary.
- ✓ Click on **Reset Location and Privacy** to delete changes made to the privacy settings and location services.

Erase an iPhone

This option will completely wipe all the settings and data on your iPhone. Remember to back up your device before you erase its content and settings.

- Tap **General** in the **Settings** app and tap the **'Reset'** option.
- Enter your Apple ID password or your iPhone passcode, and tap **Erase All Content and Settings.**

Restore iPhone from an iCloud Backup

After you have erased your device, follow the steps below to set up your device afresh, and restore content from an iCloud backup.

- Press down the Side Button until the screen lights up, and the Apple logo shows on your screen, then select your language and country.
- Click on **Set Up Manually,** select **Restore from iCloud Backup,** and then continue with the steps presented on your screen to choose an iCloud backup.

Restrict 5G

Being always on 5G will run down your battery faster. You can choose to use 5G only for video streaming. To do this,

- Tap **Cellular** in the Settings app and then click on **Cellular Data Options.**

- Click on **Voice & Data,** then choose an option:
  - ➢ **LTE** will turn off 5G completely
  - ➢ **5G Auto** will automatically switch you to LTE if the device notices that the 5G isn't providing any noticeable experience.
  - ➢ **5G On** makes 5G always available on your device.
- Tap the **Back** arrow to return to the previous screen and then click on **Data Mode** and choose an option:
  - ➢ **Low Data Mode** pauses background tasks and automatic updates to help reduce your cellular and Wi-Fi data usage.
  - ➢ **Standard** permits background tasks and automatic updates when on cellular.
  - ➢ **Allow More Data on 5G** allows you to use high data features for system tasks and apps and is usually advisable if you are on an unlimited data plan.

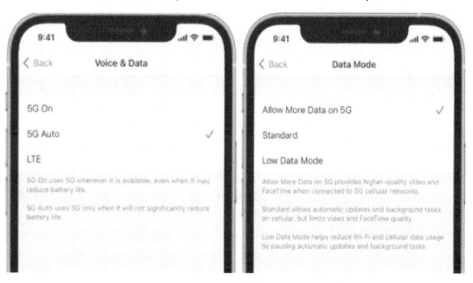

Chapter 7: Screen Time

Screen Time gives a history of how you use your device, including the websites and apps you frequently visit, how often you pick up your iPhone, and lots more. With this data, you can then decide whether to cut down on the time you spend on your device.

Set Up Screen Time

- Tap **Screen Time** in the **Settings** app, and tap '**Turn on Screen Time.**'

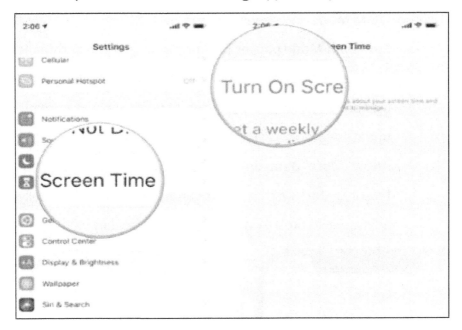

- Select **Continue** and press **This is my iPhone.**

View Your Phone Usage Data

For a report on how you use your device,

- Tap **Screen Time** in the **Settings** app, and then tap the '**See All Activity**' option.

- Click on the '**Day**' tab at the top of the screen to view a daily summary, or the '**Week**' tab to view a weekly summary.

Set Downtime

Looking at the screen time report will help you decide if you want to stay away from your device for a period. You can also block notifications and apps on your iPhone during the period. To set downtime,

- Tap **Screen Time** in the **Settings** app, and then tap **Downtime.**

- Toggle on the **'Downtime'** option on the next screen, select **Customize Days** if you want to select the days that the downtime should happen. Choose **Every Day** if you want the downtime to turn on at a selected time each day.

Set App Limits

The time limit is the amount of time per day you can access apps and apps categories. To set up,

- Tap **Screen Time** in the Settings app, and then tap **App Limits.**

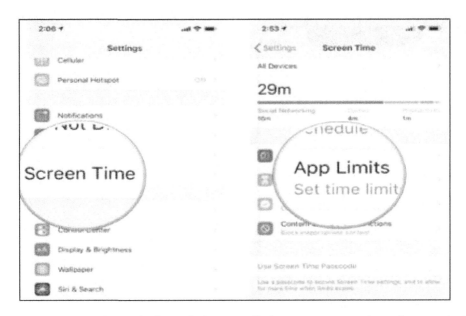

- Press **App Limit** and choose all the app categories of your choice, then press **Next.** To select different apps within a category, click on the category, and select the apps of your choice.

- Tap **Next** and allocate time for the selected apps or app categories. To select different times for each day, tap **Customize Days.**

- To add more apps or app categories, press **Choose Apps** and perform the above steps.

- After you have selected all the desired categories and apps, click **Add** to save.

Turn Off App Limits

You can choose to disable the app limit for a certain period or permanently delete the set limits.

- Tap **Screen Time** in the **Settings** app, and then tap **App Limits.**

- Select a category and tap **App Limit** to put off the limit temporarily.

- Select **Delete Limit** to permanently remove the limit from that category.

Set Communication Limits

Stop every form of communication, including messages and phone calls, from selected contacts on your device, either during certain periods or at all times.

You will need to turn on the **Contacts** option first:

- Tap your name in the Settings app, select **iCloud,** then turn on **Contacts.**

- Tap **Screen Time** in the Settings app and then tap the 'Communication Limits' option.

- To limit communication when Downtime is in effect, select **During Downtime,** or select **During Screen Time** to apply the communication limit at any time. Then select an option on your screen:
  - ➢ Contacts & Groups with at Least One Contact
  - ➢ Contacts Only
  - ➢ Everyone

Choose Apps You Want to be Always Available

See below steps on selecting apps that should be available at all times, regardless of any downtime or restriction on your device.

- Tap **Screen Time** in the Settings app, and then press **Always Allowed.**

- Tap to remove an app from the list of **Allowed Apps,** or to add an app to the list.

How to Create Content and Privacy Restrictions

Set restrictions for iTunes and App Store purchases as well as block offensive content on your device.

- Tap **Screen Time** in the **Settings** app and then tap the '**Content & Privacy Restrictions'** option.
- Move the switch beside '**Content & Privacy Restrictions'** to the right to turn it on.
- Then click **Options** to choose content allowances for the different options on your screen.

Chapter 8: Face ID

Use the Face ID to secure your apps and unlock your device just by staring into your iPhone. You can also use the Face ID to authenticate payments and purchases on iTunes, App Store & other third-party apps. Before you can set up Face ID, you need to create a passcode on your device.

Create a Passcode

A passcode is an alternative way of securing your phone and its content.

- Tap **Face ID and Passcode** in the Settings app, then tap the '**Turn Passcode On**' option.

- Enter your preferred 6-digit passcode or click on **Passcode Options** to choose either a custom alphanumeric code, custom numeric code, or a four-digit code.

- Enter the new passcode again to complete.

Set Up Face ID

After setting up the passcode on your device, follow the steps below to register Face ID:

- Click **Face ID & Passcode** in the **Settings** app and enter your device passcode on the next screen.

- Click on **Set up Face ID,** then press '**Get Started**' and continue with the instructions presented on your screen to finish.

Set up Alternate Appearance

Use this option to create an additional appearance for unlocking your device

- Click **Face ID & Passcode** in the **Settings** app and enter your device passcode on the next screen.

- Tap the **'Set up an Alternate Appearance'** option, then continue with the instructions presented on your screen to finish.

Disable Face ID

To turn off Face ID,

- Click **Face ID & Passcode** in the **Settings** app and enter your device passcode on the next screen.

- Tap the **'Reset Face ID'** option to disable Face ID.

- You can also choose not to use Face ID for certain features like Apple Pay, Safari Autofill, and lots more. Toggle off the switch for the options you do not want.

Chapter 9: Find My

Find My is an app that you can use to share your location with family and friends, erase missing devices, track down and remotely lock your lost devices, amongst other options.

Set Up Share Your Location

Use this option to set up Location sharing to share your location with others.

- Launch **Find My** on your device and click the **'Me'** tab at the bottom.

- Move the switch beside **'Share My Location'** to the right to turn it on. Move the switch to the left to stop sharing your location.

- Scroll to the end of the screen and then tap **Use this iPhone as My Location,** if displayed.

Share Your Location

To allow others to view your current location,

- Click the **People** tab at the bottom of the **Find My** app.
- Tap **Share My Location** close to the end of the screen and then tap the ⊕ button in the **To** field to choose a contact. You may also manually enter the name of the contact in the **To** field.
- Tap **Send** and choose how long the receiver should access your location.

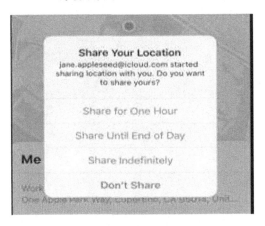

Stop Sharing your Location with a Friend

Hide your location from one or more friends.

- Click the **People** tab at the bottom of the Find My app.
- Select a friend from the displayed list and tap the '**Stop Sharing My Location**' option.
- Then select **Stop Sharing Location** to finish.

Remove a Friend

Remove a friend from the list of people that can view your location.

- Launch Find My on your device and click the **People** tab at the bottom.
- Select a friend from the displayed list and tap **Remove [name].**
- Select **Remove** to complete.

Respond to a Location Sharing Request

When you receive a request to share your location, you may do the following:

- Click the **People** tab at the bottom of the Find My app.
- Scroll to the contact that sent the request and tap **Share** underneath the name. Then select the length of the sharing period.
- You may also tap **Cancel** to deny access to your location.

Stop Receiving Location Sharing Request

To prevent your contacts from requesting your location,

- Launch Find My on your device and click the **Me** tab at the bottom.
- Now move the switch beside **'Allow Friend Requests'** to the left to turn it off.

Ask a Friend to Share their Location

Just like a friend can request to view your location, you may also request to view a friend's location.

- Launch Find My on your device and click the **People** tab.

- Tap a name from the list, then tap the **'Ask to Follow Location'** option. You will only view the location of friends that permit you to view their location.

See Your Friend's Location

- Launch Find My on your device and click the **People** tab.
- Tap a name from the list to see their current location on the map.

Get Direction to a Friend

- Launch Find My on your device and click the **People** tab.
- Tap a name from the list and tap **Directions** to open Map.
- Tap the route to get directions to the location of your friend.

Notify a Friend When Your Location Changes

Let your friends or family who are iPhone users receive a notification when you move from one location to another.

- Launch Find My on your device and click the **People** tab.
- Tap a name from the list, then click **Add** under **Notifications.**
- Click on **Notify [Friend's Name],** then choose to notify your friend either at your departure or arrival.
- Choose a location on your screen or click **New Location** to add a different location.
- Select how often your friend should receive the notification, then click on **Add.**

Add your iPhone to Find My

Add all your Apple devices to Find My for easy tracking of missing devices. To add your iPhone 12,

- Tap your name in the Settings app and tap the '**Find My**' option.

- Select **Find My (device name),** then switch on **Find My (device).**

- Then turn on the '**Send Last Location**' and '**Find My network or Enable Offline Finding**' options.

Find a Missing Device

To see the location of any device that is set up on Find My,

- Launch Find My on your device and click the **Device** tab.

- Select the missing device to view its location on the map. If the device is offline, you will receive the **No Location Found** message

Play a Sound on Your Missing Device

Let's assume you lost your device within the house and need to find it urgently. You can use another of your Apple device to find the missing iPhone. The iPhone will make sounds to help you locate it.

- Launch Find My on your device and click the **Device** tab.

- Tap the missing device and click **Play Sound.** The missing device will begin to make sounds in increasing volume. You will receive a **Sound Pending** message if the iPhone is offline.

- When you find the iPhone, press the power or volume buttons to stop playing the sound.

Mark a Device as Lost

Putting your missing device on Lost Mode will prevent others from accessing the content of your iPhone

- Launch Find My on your device, click the **Device** tab, and then click on the missing device.

- Tap **Activate** under the '**Mark as Lost**' section.

- Tap **Continue** and enter your phone number if you like.

- Tap **Next** and enter a note for whoever may find the missing device. Then tap **Activate.**

Get Directions to a Device

To find your way to the location of your missing device,

- Launch Find My on your device, click the **Device** tab, and then click on the missing device.

- Click **Directions,** and Maps will open. Then click a route to get navigation to the device location.

Remotely Erase a Device

Erase all the content on your missing device to prevent third-party access

- Launch Find My on your device, click the **Device** tab and then select the missing device.

- Tap the '**Erase This Device**' option, then press **Erase This (iPhone).**

- Enter your phone number if you like and tap **Next.**

- Enter a note for whoever may find the missing device, and then tap **Erase.**

- Input your Apple ID password and press **Erase** to finish.

Cancel an Erase

If you attempt to erase a device that is offline, the remote erase will only happen after the device gets connected to a cellular or Wi-Fi network. You may choose to cancel the request before the device comes online.

- Tap the **Devices** tab and choose the device.

- Then click **Cancel Erase** and input your Apple ID password.

Chapter 10: Control Center

Control Center gives you immediate access to essential settings like screen brightness, hotspot, airplane mode, and lots more.

Open Control Center

- Swipe down from the upper right part of your screen to go to the control center. Swipe up to exit.

Add and Organize Controls

Add more app shortcuts to your Control center – apps like Voice Memos, Notes, etc.

- Tap **Control Center** in the Settings app, then scroll through the available controls.

- Tap the ⊕ button to add a control, or tap the ⊖ button to remove a control or shortcut.

- Reorder the position of the controls – press the ≡ button beside a control and then move the control up or down on the list.

Enable or Disable Wi-Fi

- Go to the Control Center and tap the 📶 button to turn on Wi-Fi. Tap the 📶 button to turn it off.

Enable or Disable Bluetooth

- Go to the Control Center and tap the button to turn on Bluetooth. Tap the button to turn it off.

Turn off Access to Control Center from within Apps

By default, you can access the control center from any screen on your iPhone. However, you can turn off the 'Access within Apps' options:

- Tap **Control Center** in the Settings app, then turn off the **'Access Within Apps'** switch.

Chapter 11: Add Widgets to your Home Screen

On the 'Today View' widget, you will find up-to-date info from several apps on your iPhone, items like calendar events, weather reports, and lots more. This widget is not on the home screen by default; you will need to move it to the home screen to quickly and easily view all this information.

Open Today View

- Make a swipe right from the left edge of your Lock Screen or Home Screen. To go to the home screen, swipe up from the bottom end of your screen.

Move a Widget to your Home Screen

See below how to move widgets from the Today View screen to your home screen:

- Open 'Today View' and press firmly on a desired widget to get it to jiggle.
- Now pull the widget off the right side of your screen and place it in any part of the Home screen.
- Tap **Done** to finish.

Add a Widget to your Home Screen

To add a widget to one of the pages on your home screen,

- Swipe to the desired home screen page, then touch and hold the screen until your apps start jiggling.
- Tap at the upper part of your screen, then look for a widget you like, click it, then scroll left to see the different sizes.

- Once you get to a size you like, tap **Add Widget** to add it to your home screen, then tap **Done.**

Customize a Widget

Edit individual widgets to only show you the information you want to see. For instance, you can customize the Weather widget to show the weather forecast for a location outside your immediate environment.

- Go to the home screen (swipe up from the bottom end of your screen), and press firmly on a widget to launch the 'Quick Actions' option.

- Click on **Edit Widget** or **Edit Stack,** and select an option that suits you. Tap the home screen to save.

Remove a Widget from your Home Screen

- Go to the home screen (swipe up from the bottom end of your screen), and press firmly on a widget to launch the 'Quick Actions' option.

- Select either **Remove Widget** or **Remove Stack,** then press **Remove.**

Access Today View when iPhone is Locked

Before you can access Today View on your lock screen, you will need to configure the settings.

- Tap **Face ID & Passcode** in the **Settings** app on your device.

- Input your passcode, then turn on the switch for **Today View.**

Chapter 12: Share Content with AirDrop

Apple users can wirelessly send their videos, photos, locations, and more to other nearby Apple devices using AirDrop. You need to be signed in with your Apple ID, then turn on Bluetooth and Wi-Fi before this feature can work.

Send an Item using AirDrop

To share an item using AirDrop,

- Open the item and tap the ⬆️ or ●●● icons, **AirDrop, Share,** or any other app sharing option on your screen.

- Tap the 📶 button in the row of share options, and then tap the profile image of another AirDrop user nearby.

- If the receiver uses an iPhone 11 or 12 models, you may point your device towards their device, then tap their profile image at the upper part of your screen.

- If you experience difficulty locating the receiver, you may ask them to go to their control center and permit **AirDrop** to receive shared items.

Allow Others to Send items to Your iPhone Using AirDrop

Before you can receive items from other iPhone users, you will need to set up the option on your iPhone.

- Swipe down from the upper right side of your screen to go to the control center, then tap 📶 .

- Choose **Contacts Only** to only receive from contacts stored on your phone or click on **Everyone** to receive from even those not saved on your iPhone.

Receive a Password

A sender must have your details stored in their contact before they can share passwords with you. To receive,

- First, allow AirDrops to receive items.
- Then tap **Accept** when you get the request to accept a password from a sender.

The password is automatically saved on your iPhone. You can then view it and also use it on the sign-in screen for the compatible apps.

Send a Password using AirDrop

Share passwords securely to other Apple device users who are in your Contacts. The receiver must allow AirDrop to receive items for this to work.

- Tap **Passwords** in the **Settings** app and select an account you wish to share.
- Click **Password** and select **AirDrop** in the pop-up menu.
- Select a contact on your screen to send the password.

Chapter 13: Use iPhone to Search

Quickly find contacts and apps, search and open webpages, search inside apps like Messages as well as start a web search with the 'Search on iPhone' option. Here is how to use this option:

- Swipe up from the bottom end of your screen to go to the Home screen, then swipe down from the middle of your screen.

- Click on the search field and fill in your search phrase, then tap **Go** on your keyboard to display the search results.
- Click on any result to view more details or launch the app.

- Tap ⊗ to start a new search.

Choose Apps to Include in Search

- Tap **Siri & Search** in the **Settings** app, then touch an app and turn the switch beside '**Show in Search**' on or off to enable or disable.

Search inside Apps

Certain apps allow you to search within the app.

- Open the app and locate the search field or the 🔍 button.

- Then enter a search phrase and click **Search.**

Turn off Siri Suggestions in Search

When you search on your iPhone, you will also find some Siri suggestions relating to your search phrase. You can turn off Siri suggestions below:

- Tap **Siri & Search** in the Settings app, then move the switch beside '**Suggestions in Search**' to the left to disable it.

Chapter 14: Screenshots and Screen Recording

Take a screenshot of your screen or record actions on your screen and use it in a document or share it with a third party.

Take a Screenshot

- At the same time, press and release both the Side and Volume up buttons.

- The screenshot thumbnail will appear at the bottom left side of your screen. Click on the thumbnail and tap **Done.**

- Then choose what you want to do with the screenshot: **Delete Screenshot, Save to Photos** or **Save to Files.**

Screen Recording

Capture actions on your screen and include sounds and audio to your recording.

- Tap **Control Center** in the Settings app, scroll to **Screen Recording,** and tap the ⊕ button beside it.

- Swipe down from the upper right part of your screen to go to the control center, tap ◉ and your screen will begin to record after the 3-second countdown.

- To add sound to your recording, touch and hold the ◉ icon, then select **Microphone.**

- When you are satisfied with your screen recording, go to the control center and tap ◉ , then click **Stop.**

- Your screen recordings are stored in the Photos app.

Chapter 15: App Library and Home Screen

iOS 14 introduces the new App Library. While the Home screen organizes all your apps into different pages, the App Library organizes all your apps in a simple, easy-to-navigate pattern.

App Library

The App Library shows you all your apps according to their categories. For example, to view all your social apps, go to the App Library, and tap **Social.** Here is how to access the App Library:

- Swipe up from the bottom end of your screen to go to the Home screen, then swipe left till you get past the Home screen pages.

- Click on a category to view all the apps inside the category or tap the Search space at the upper part of your screen to search for an app. Click on an app to launch it.

- You can have an app on your App Library without having the app on your home screen. To add the app to the home screen, touch and hold the app until you see a pop-up, then tap the **'Add to Home Screen'** option.

Open Apps on Home Screen

To view all the apps on your home screen pages,

- Go to the home screen – swipe up from the bottom end of your screen.

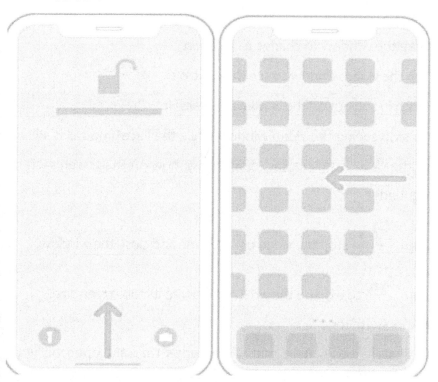

- Then move through the different home screen pages to view all the apps on the home screen.

- Swipe up from the bottom end of your screen to go back to the first home screen page.

- Tap an app icon to open the app.

Multitask with Picture-in-Picture

Picture-in-Picture lets you make a FaceTime call or play a video and use other apps simultaneously.

- Play a video or begin a FaceTime call, then tap on your screen to reduce the video window size and show the home screen.

- Open an app from the home screen if desired.

- Drag the window to change its location.

- Tap the video window to see the controls.

- Pinch in and out on the window to resize it.

- To stop seeing the video window while the FaceTime call is still on or the video is still playing, drag the window off the screen's left or right edge.

- Tap to stop the video or FaceTime and close the window.

- Tap to expand the video window to its full-screen size.

Use the App Switcher

The App Switcher will show you all the apps that are open on your device.

- From any screen, swipe up from the bottom end of the screen and stop in the middle of the screen.

- This will open the App switcher to see all your open apps. Swipe left or right, then tap an app to go to it.

Switch Between Open Apps

Here is one quick way to switch between the open apps on your device:

- Swipe left or right by the bottom end of your device screen.

Quit an App

To close an app,

- Open the App switcher and swipe till you get to the app, then make a swipe-up gesture on the app to close it.

- You can always re-open the app from the home screen or App library.

Delete an App

Permanently delete an app from your iPhone.

- Swipe to the app on the home screen or app library, touch and hold it, tap **Delete App,** then tap **Delete.**

Remove Apps from Home Screen

Remove an app from your home screen page and keep the app in the App library.

- Go to your home screen and locate the app you want to remove.

- Then touch and hold the app until you see a pop-up menu.

- Tap **Remove App** and select **Move to App Library.**

Chapter 16: Apple Pay

Apple Pay is a contactless payment technology available on all Apple devices, created to encourage users to pay using their device rather than a debit or credit card. You can use Apple Pay to make a payment on apps, sites, and stores, as well as receive and send money.

Set Up Apple Pay

Here is how to set up Apple Pay for the first time:

- Open the Wallet app and click the ⊕ button.

- To add a new card, position your device camera to capture the details in front of your card. You may also enter the details manually on the screen.

- If you have created Apple Pay on another device, you will find all your existing cards on the app. Click on a card you want to add to your iPhone, tap **Continue,** and then enter the card's CVV.

Choose Your Default Card

Any card that was added first to the Wallet app will automatically serve as the default card. To change the default card,

- Scroll to the new card you want to use as your default in the Wallet app, tap and hold the card and then move it to the top of the stack.
- Once the card comes on top as the first card, it automatically becomes your new default card.

Make Contactless Payment with your Default Card

To make payment at a physical location,

- Press the side button twice to see the default card.
- Then enter your passcode or authenticate using the Face ID.
- Now place the top of your device within some centimeters away from the contactless reader.
- When the payment is complete, you will see a checkmark on your screen.

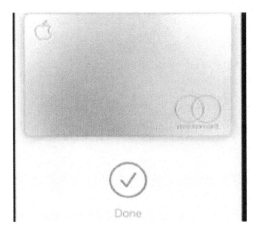

Pay with a Different Card

You can also make your payments using a card that is not the default card.

- Press the side button twice to see the default card.
- Tap the default card to bring up other cards, then select another card.
- Approve your transaction using either passcode or Face ID.
- Now place the top of your device within some centimeters away from the contactless reader.
- When the payment is complete, you will see a checkmark on your screen.

Make Online Payments

You can also use this service to make payments on the web, in an app, or an app clip.

- Open the web or app and initiate your transaction.
- Tap the **Apple Pay** button when it's time to pay for your purchase.
- Go through the payment info, press the side button twice and then approve the transaction using either passcode or Face ID.

Change Your Shipping and Contact Details

- Tap **Wallet & Apple Pay** in the **Settings** app, then select an option on your screen to change it.

Delete a Card from Apple Pay

- Tap **Wallet & Apple Pay** in the Settings app, tap the card, then scroll down and select **Remove this Card.**

Here is another way to delete a card from Apple Wallet:

- Click the card in the Wallet app, tap the 3-dot ⚫ icon, and then select **Remove this Card.**

Modify your Apple Pay Settings

- Tap **Wallet & Apple Pay** in the Settings app and choose your preferred options on the next screen:

- Tap the **'Double-Click Side Button'** option if you want to see your cards when you tap the Side button twice.

- Tap the **'Allow Payments on Mac'** option to initiate a transaction on your Mac and make the payment on your iPhone.

Set Up Apple Cash

Apple device users can send and receive money via the Messages app. The received amount is credited to your Apple Cash card in the Wallet app. You may then choose to transfer your Apple cash balance to your bank or spend directly on the Wallet app.

- Tap **Wallet & Apple Pay** in the Settings app and then turn on the switch for **Apple Cash.**

Manage your Apple Cash

- Tap the Apple Cash card in the Wallet app to see your most recent transactions.

- Then press the button to request for your statement, see your suggested PIN, contact Apple Support, and so on.

Request Payment

- Open an iMessage conversation in Messages, then click and enter an amount.

- Click **Request,** then send your message.

Send Payment in Messages

- Open an iMessage conversation in Messages, then click and enter an amount.

- Click **Pay,** enter a note if you want, then tap the button.

- Go through the payment information before you authorize the payment using your passcode or Face ID.

Chapter 17: FaceTime

Make FaceTime audio or video calls to other Apple device users.

Set Up FaceTime

- Press **FaceTime** in the Settings app, then turn on the **'FaceTime'** switch.

- Toggle on **FaceTime Live Photos** so that you can capture Live Photos when making video calls.

- Enter your email address, Apple ID, or the phone number you wish to use with FaceTime.

Make a FaceTime Call

- Tap the ╪ button at the top right side of the FaceTime app, then input the number of the person you want to call.

- Then press ▭◁ to make a video call or ☎ to make an audio call.

- If the call goes unanswered, you can choose to **Leave a Message, Call Back** or **Cancel** the call.

- If the receiver picked the call, tap ✕ to end at any time.

To initiate the call from your FaceTime call history

- Open FaceTime and scroll through the history tap, then tap the person you want to call.

Start a FaceTime Call from a Message Conversation

While chatting with a friend in the Message app,

- Click the profile image  or name of the friend at the top of the conversation, then select the **'FaceTime'** option.

Receive FaceTime Call

When a FaceTime call comes in, you will find the below options on your screen:

Set up a reminder to return the call later.

Send the caller a text message.

- Tap **Decline** to reject the call or **Accept** to speak with the caller.
- Tap **Message** to decline and message the caller.

- Tap **Remind Me** to decline and set a reminder to return the call at a later time.

- If you are on an active call and receive a new call, you can choose to '**End and Accept**' the new call or '**Hold and Accept.**' The '**End and Accept**' option will drop the existing call and switch to the new caller.

Make FaceTime HD Calls

iPhone 12 allows for FaceTime video calls in 1080p HD. To set it up,

- Tap **Cellular** in the Settings app, click the '**Data Mode**' option, and tap '**Allow More Data on 5G.**'

Delete a Call from Your Call History

- Go through the call history in the FaceTime app until you find a call you want to delete, swipe left on the call, and tap **Delete.**

Start a Group FaceTime Call

Call more than one person at once.

- Tap the ┼ button at the top right side of the FaceTime app, then input the numbers of everyone you want on the call.

- Press ▭◁ to make a video call or ☎ to make an audio call.

- If the call goes unanswered, you can choose to **Leave a Message, Call Back** or **Cancel** the call.

- If the receivers picked the call, tap ⊗ to end at any time.

Customize the FaceTime Tile for Group Call

When a participant speaks in a group FaceTime call, the tile for the speaker grows bigger than the tile for other participants. If you do not like this setting, follow the steps below to change it:

- Tap **FaceTime** in the settings app and then disable the '**Speaking**' option under the **Automatic Prominence** section.
- Everyone will not have equal tile.

Take Live Photo in FaceTime

While making a FaceTime video call, you can capture a photo of the other person(s).

- On a call with a single person, tap the ⭕ button. On a group call, tap the participant's tile, press ⬉ , and then press ⭕ .
- You, as well as the other party, will get a notification of the Live Photo.

Turn FaceTime Eye Contact On or Off

This setting makes it look as if you are staring into the eyes of the other party during a FaceTime video call. To enable or disable,

- Tap **FaceTime** in the Settings app and then turn the '**Eye Contact**' switch on or off.

Change FaceTime Video and Audio Settings

When making or receiving a FaceTime call, touch your device screen to display the controls that you can use for the call.

- Tap 🎤 to mute the call.

- Tap ⟳ to switch from the front to the back camera or the back to the front camera.

- To turn off your camera during a video call, swipe up from the top part of the control and select the '**Camera Off**' option.

Switch to a Message Conversation

Move your conversation from FaceTime to Messages.

- Touch your device screen to display the call controls, swipe up from above the controls, and then tap 💬.

Block Unwanted Callers in FaceTime

Block calls and messages from unwanted people.

- Press **FaceTime** in the Settings app, and select **Blocked Contacts.**

- Move close to the bottom of your screen and tap **Add New.**

- Then select all the unwanted people in your Contacts.

- To unblock a phone number or contact, swipe left on the contact, then select **Unblock.**

Chapter 18: Messages on iPhone 12

There are two ways to communicate using the Messages app – send text messages as the regular SMS/MMS, or send iMessage to other Apple device users.

Sign in to iMessage

- Tap **Messages** in the Settings app, then turn on the **'iMessage'** switch.

Send a Message

- Open an existing conversation or press the [✎] button at the top right side of your screen to begin a new conversation.

- Enter the receiver's details if starting a new conversation, enter your message in the text field, and tap the **Send** [↑] button to deliver your message.

- A [!] button will appear if the delivery was unsuccessful. Tap the button to resend the message.

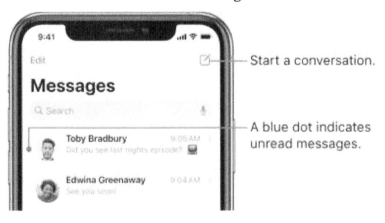

Start a conversation.

A blue dot indicates unread messages.

- Swipe left on a conversation to see when you sent the message or when the message was delivered.

Reply to a Message

- Open a conversation in Messages, type your message in the text field, and then tap the **Send** button to deliver your message.

Share Your Name and Profile Image

When sending or responding to a message in Messages, you can choose to share your name and profile image with the other party. The first time you launch the Messages app, you will need to enter your name and choose your profile photo.

You can then change your profile photo, name, or sharing options at any time with the steps below:

- Tap the button in Messages, then select **Edit Name & Photo.**
- Click the space that has your current name & enter the new name.
- To change your profile image, tap **Edit,** and select a new image.
- To stop sharing your name and image, turn off the '**Name and Photo Sharing'** switch. Turn on the switch to resume sharing.
- To select the persons that can view your name and image, scroll to **Share Automatically,** and choose the appropriate option.
- Then tap **Done** at the top right side of your screen.

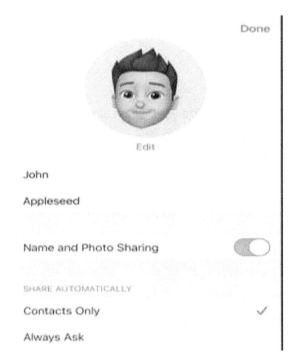

Done

Edit

John

Appleseed

Name and Photo Sharing

SHARE AUTOMATICALLY

Contacts Only ✓

Always Ask

Pin a Conversation

Any conversation that you pin will stay at the top of the Messages list, regardless of the time that the message was sent or received.

- Scroll to the conversation you want, swipe right, and tap 📌.

Unpin a Conversation

To remove the pinned conversation from the top of the list,

- Tap and hold the conversation, then select 📌.

Switch from Messages to FaceTime

Transfer to a FaceTime call while chatting in the Messages app.

- Click the name or profile image of the contact you are chatting with in **Messages**, then tap the **'FaceTime'** option.

Reply to a Specific Message in a Group Conversation

Reply to a single message in a group conversation.

- Touch and hold the message you want to reply to in the group

  conversation, then tap .

- Type your message and tap the **Send** button to deliver your

  message.

Mention Someone in a Group Conversation

When you mention someone in a group conversation in iMessage, they get

notified depending on their settings.

- Type @ followed by the contact's name, type your message, and tap

  .

Receive Notification when Mentioned

To get a notification of a mention in a group conversation,

- Tap **Message** in the Settings app and tap the **'Notify Me'** option.

Send Videos or Photos in a Conversation

- Open an existing or a new message, write your message in the text

  field, then tap .

- Click the shutter button to take a photo, or switch to **Video**

  mode and tap to record video.

- To insert an image or photo from the Photos app, tap in the app

  drawer and choose a photo on the next screen.

- Tap the **Send** ⬆ button or the ⊗ button to cancel.

Edit or Mark-Up a Photo

You can write, draw, or edit a picture before you insert it into your message.

- Open an existing or a new message, tap the 🌸 button, and select a photo.

- Tap **Edit,** and then use the editing tools on your screen to draw, write, or edit the photo. Tap **Done** to save.

- To markup the photo, tap **Markup** at the center top of your screen, then make every necessary editing and tap **Done.**

- Tap the **Send** ⬆ button or the ✕ button to cancel.

Send an Audio Message

To send an audio recording to your receiver,

- Open an existing conversation or a new message, then touch and hold the 🔊 icon to start recording your message.

- Tap ▶ to listen to the recording.

- Tap the **Send** ⬆ button or the ✕ button to cancel.

Listen and Reply to an Audio Message

- When you receive an audio message, raise your iPhone to your ear, and the audio will begin playing.

- Raise the phone again to make your audio reply.

The 'Raise to Listen' feature is enabled by default. To turn it off,

- Tap **Messages** in the Settings app, then turn off the '**Raise to Listen**' switch.

Manage Attachments in Messages

You can forward, save, copy, delete, or print attachments in a conversation.

- To forward a message or its attachment, press and hold the message or the attachment, click on **More,** choose other items you want to forward, then tap ➥ .

- To save, print, or share an attachment, open the attachment and tap ⬆ .

- To erase a message or its attachment, press and hold the message or the attachment, click on **More,** choose other items you want to delete, then tap  .

- To copy an attachment, press and hold the attachment, then click **Copy.**

Send Handwritten Messages

Use your finger to write your message, and it will appear exactly the same way to the receiver.

- Open an existing conversation or a new message, then switch your device to landscape mode.

Scroll to write a
longer message.

Clear   Done

thank you

hello   thank you   happy birthday   congratulations   thinking of you   I'm sorry

Choose a saved message.   Return to the
Touch and hold to delete   keyboard.
a saved message.

- Tap ✐ on the keyboard and write your message using your fingers. Tap **Done** & the message will be saved at the bottom edge

98

of the handwriting screen for future use. Click on a saved message to use it.

- Tap the **Send** ⬆ button or the ⊗ button to cancel.

- To delete saved messages, press & hold the message, then tap ⊗

Create a Memoji

Memoji are animations that mirror your facial expressions and mimics your voice. You can personalize your Memoji by changing the hairstyle and color, skin color, facial expressions, and lots more.

- Open an existing conversation or a new message, press the Memoji button, then press ✛.

- Now customize the Memoji to your taste and tap **Done** to save.

Edit a Memoji

To delete, edit or duplicate a Memoji you created,

- Open an existing conversation or a new message, and press the Memoji button.

- Tap a Memoji and then press ⋯.

- Then choose to **Duplicate, Delete,** or **Edit.**

Use Memoji and Memoji Stickers in a Conversation

After you create a Memoji, your device will make different Memoji sticker packs using the Memoji you created. You can then use the stickers to reply or send a message.

- Open a conversation or new message, press the Memoji icon, then click a Memoji at the top row to view its stickers.

- Click on a sticker to include it in your conversation before you send your message.

Send Memoji Recordings

To send a Memoji that mirrors your facial expressions and talks like you,

- Open a conversation or new message, press , then click the Memoji you want to use.

- Tap the button to begin recording your voice and facial expressions. Once done, tap to stop recording.

- Click **Replay** to view the message, then tap the **Send** button or the Delete button to cancel.

Share Your Location in Messages

To send your current location to someone in your family sharing group,

- Open a conversation with your desired receiver, then click their profile image or name.

- Press and select an option on your screen.

Download and Use iMessage Apps

Share songs, play games, decorate your conversation with stickers right on the Messages app. To enjoy these features, you may need to download more iMessage apps from the iOS app store.

- Click on a conversation, then tap to launch the app store.

Browse iMessage apps.

- Go through the different iMessage apps on your screen, click to see more about the app, then click GET to download the app if it is a free app, or press the app price to download paid apps.

- After you have downloaded an app, go to a conversation in Messages and click the iMessage app in the app drawer.

- Tap a content in the app to add it to your message, type your message, then tap the **Send** button or the button to cancel.

Chapter 19: Siri

Siri helps to get things done quickly – from getting a weather report to translating a word and lots more.

Set Up Siri

- Tap **Siri & Search** in the Settings app, then turn on the switch for **Listen for "Hey Siri"** (this option allows you to summon Siri by saying "Hey Siri," followed by your request or question).

- Turn on the switch for **Press Side Button for Siri** (this option allows you to summon Siri by pressing the side button). To use this option, press and hold the side button and ask your question or request when you see Siri on your screen.

- Tap to ask another question or make a different request.

Type to Siri

Siri not only hears you but can also read you. To type your request or question, you need to set up the option.

- Press **Accessibility** in the Settings app and tap **Siri.**
- Then turn on the switch for **'Type to Siri.'**
- To use this option, first, summon Siri using any method of your choice, then type your question in the text space on your screen.

Let Siri Know You

Siri uses the information you fill in the My Cards tab to personalize services for you. These include details like your home and work addresses, your relationships, and lots more.

- Open the Contacts app on your device, then press **My Card** at the top of your screen.

- Tap **Edit** and enter all the required details.

- If you can't find any card, press ╋ , and then enter your details.

- Once done, go to the Settings app, click **Contacts,** select **My Info,** then click on your name on the list.

- Then return to the Settings app and tap **Siri & Search,** select **My Information,** then click on your name on the list.

Allow Siri when Locked

To use Siri on your locked screen, follow the steps below:

- Tap **Siri & Search** in the Settings app, then turn on the '**Allow Siri when Locked'** switch. Turn off the switch to disable the option.

- You can also change the Siri language on this screen. Tap **Language** and select the preferred language.

Hide Apps when you Summon Siri

You can summon Siri at any time, even when using an app. You can also choose to hide the active app while Siri is on the screen.

- Press **Accessibility** in the Settings app, click **Siri** and then turn off the '**Show Apps Behind Siri'** switch.

Change Siri Settings

Customize Siri to suit your needs and preference.

- Tap **Siri & Search** in the Settings app, and you will find several settings for Siri.

- To change Siri's voice, select **Siri Voice** and then change Siri accent or choose a female/ male voice for Siri.

- If you will like to see your request displayed on your screen, click **Siri Responses,** then turn on the **'Always Show Speech'** switch.

- If you like to see Siri's response displayed on your screen, click the **'Siri Responses'** option, then turn on the **'Always Show Siri Captions'** switch.

- To limit Siri's verbal response to a specific period or time, tap **Siri Responses,** and choose an option under **Spoken Responses.**

Change Siri Settings for an Individual App

To change the Siri shortcut settings or Siri suggestions for individual apps,

- Tap **Siri & Search** in the Settings app and tap the app you want.

- Then make the appropriate changes as you desire.

Adjust Siri Voice Volume

- Use the volume keys to control Siri's voice volume.

Disable Hey Siri when your Phone is Facing Down

Siri always listens for your summon even when your device is locked or facing down. To prevent Siri from responding to the Hey Siri prompt when the iPhone is covered or faced down,

- Tap **Accessibility** in the Settings app.

- Select **Siri,** then turn off the **'Always Listen for "Hey Siri"'** switch.

Chapter 20: Mail App

Write and edit your emails, receive and send documents, videos, presentations, and more.

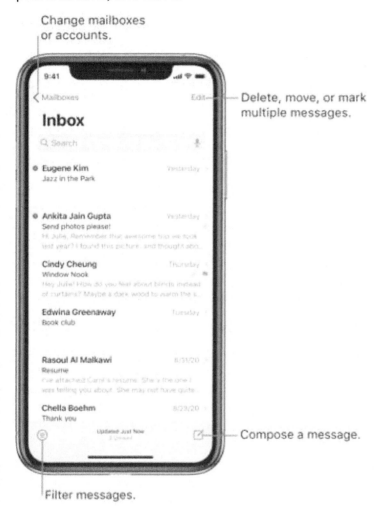

Change mailboxes or accounts.

Delete, move, or mark multiple messages.

Compose a message.

Filter messages.

Reply to an Email

- Open the email you want to respond to, then tap .

- Select **Reply,** and type your message.

- To attach a document, video, or image to the mail, tap ‹ above your keyboard, then tap ▢ to attach a document or tap 🖼 to attach a video or image. Click on the video, image, or document to attach it to the email.

- To take a new video or picture and insert it into your email, tap ‹ above your keyboard, then tap the 📷 button and capture your picture or video. Tap **Retake** to shoot again or tap **Use Video** or **Use Photo** to include the item in your email.

- Then click the **Send** ⬆ button.

Quote Some Text in Your Reply

Include some text from the sender's email for better clarity.

- Open the sender's email, press and hold the first word of the content you want to quote, & swipe to the last word in the quote.

- Tap ↩, select **Reply,** type your message and send.

Scan a Document to Your Email

- Open the email you want to respond to, then tap ↩.

- Select **Reply,** and type your message.

- Tap ‹ above the keyboard, tap ⊡, and then place the document to show on your device screen. The iPhone will automatically scan the document once it recognizes the document on your screen. Tap ⭕ or press the volume button to scan the document manually.

- Scan all the pages and tap **Save** to insert the scan in your email.
- You can always edit the document before you send – tap the document, then tap 🔵 to use a filter, tap 🗗 to crop, tap ⟲ to rotate, or tap 🗑 to delete.

Create an Email Message

- Tap 📝 at the bottom-right edge of the Mail home page.
- Enter the receiving email address in the **To** field, enter the theme of the message in the **Subject** field, then type your message in the text field.
- If you have more than one email address set up on your device, tap the **From** button to select your sending email address.
- Use the **CC** field to copy other email addresses for information's sake and the BCC field to blind copy persons you do not want others to see.
- Tap ⬆ to deliver your email to the receiver.

Draw in Your Email

- Open the email you want to respond to, tap ↩, & select **Reply.**

- Click on the message field, tap ⟨ above the onscreen keyboard, then click Ⓐ in the format bar.

- Select a color or tool from the buttons close to the bottom of your screen, then write or draw as you want.

- Tap **Done** and select **Insert Drawing.** Send your email once done.

Search for an Email

The Mail app has more than one criteria that you can use to search for emails. You can use text, timeframe, or email attributes.

- Open Mails and go to a Mailbox, then swipe down to the center of the page to display the Search space.

- Tap the search space and then enter your search phrase or when the mail was sent or received. You may also enter an email attribute like "flagged," "unread," "attachment," etc.

- Select if you want the search to include all your mailboxes or just the current mailbox.

Add Mail Accounts

To create mail accounts on your device,

- Tap **Mail** in the Settings app and select **Add Account.**

- Press **Other** and tap the '**Add Mail Account'** option.

- Enter the new email address and password, then tap **Next.**

- Enter every other requested info on the next screen, & tap **Save.**

Automatically Send a Copy to Yourself

To always receive a copy of every email that you send,

- Tap **Mail** in the Settings app and then turn on the '**Always BCC Myself'** switch.

Create Your Email Signature

Include your signature in all the emails you send.

- Tap **Mail** in the Settings app and then select **Signature.**
- Tap the text space at the top of your screen and set up your signature.
- If you have more than one email address and will like to use different signatures for each mail account, tap the **'Per Account'** option and follow the onscreen steps to create signatures per account.

Show a Longer Preview

When you receive a new mail, you will see the first two text lines for that email. You can increase the preview to show up to five lines.

- Tap **Mail** in the Settings app and then select **Preview.**
- Choose the applicable option on the next screen.

Show the CC and To Labels

To display the CC & To labels,

- Tap **Mail** in the Settings app and then turn on the '**Show To/Cc Labels'** switch.

You may also create a To/CC mailbox to view all the mails addressed to you.

- Open the Mail app, click on **Mailboxes,** select **Edit,** then choose **To or CC.**

Add a Contact from Received Email

To save a contact from the email they sent to you,

- Click the name or email address of the sender, then select **Add to Existing Contacts,** or **Create New Contact** and fill in the necessary details.

Flag an Email

Flag emails that you wish to attend to in the nearest future – the email will stay in the 'inbox' and 'flagged' mailbox. To flag an email,

- Tap ⤺ inside an email and select **Flag.**

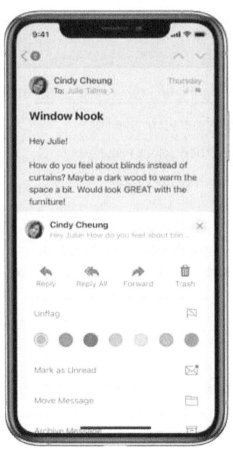

- Choose a color for the flag if desired.

- To unflag an email, tap ⬋ inside the flagged email & tap **Unflag** ⚑ close to the page's bottom.

To access your flagged emails,

- Tap **Mailboxes** by your left**,** tap **Edit,** and tap the '**Flagged'** option.

Receive Email Notification

Create mail notifications when sending or reading an email.

- When sending an email, touch the Subject field and tap 🔔 the icon in that field, then tap the '**Notify Me'** option.

- Or open a received email, tap ⬋ and select **Notify Me.**

Mute Email Notifications

Mute email notifications from a single thread in Mails.

- Tap ⬋ inside the desired email, then select **Mute.**

You can also decide what should happen with the muted emails.

- Press **Mail** in the Settings app, tap the '**Muted Thread Action'** option, and choose an option.

Block Contacts

Block an email address from sending you emails.

- Open an email from a sender, touch the email address, and then tap '**Block This Contact.'**

Manage Junk Email

To move an email from your inbox to the junk folder,

- Tap ⟵ inside the desired email, then select **Move to Junk.**
- To undo your action, quickly swipe left with your three fingers.

Manage Emails with a Swipe

While on the Mail home page, you can swipe to mark an email as read, send to trash, and more.

- Slowly swipe to the left of an email until you can see the menu, then select an option.

To choose options that should pop up when you swipe on an email,

- Press **Mail** in the Settings app and tap '**Swipe Options.**'

Reorder Your Mailboxes

Place your frequently used mailbox at the top of the Mailboxes list.

- Open Mails and click **Mailboxes** at the top left.

- Select **Edit,** press the hamburger ☰ icon beside a mailbox until it lifts, then move the mailbox to a new location.

Mark or Move Multiple Emails

- Open Mails and click **Edit,** select all the emails you want, and then choose an action for the selected emails.
- To undo your action, quickly swipe left with your three fingers.

Delete Emails

See below all the different ways to delete an email in Mails.

- Open an email and tap 🗑 at the end of the page.

- Open Mails, go through the mail list, then swipe left on an email and select **Trash** from the options.

- To delete multiple emails at the same time, open Mails, tap **Edit,** select all the emails you want, then press **Trash.**

- To undo your action, quickly swipe left with your three fingers.

Confirm Email Deletion

When you attempt to delete an email or emails, Mail will ask you to confirm your decision. To stop this confirmation request,

- Press **Mail** in Settings, then turn off the **'Ask Before Deleting'** switch. Turn the switch on to continue getting the confirmation requests.

Recovered Deleted Emails

- Open the Trash mailbox in Mails, open the mail you want to recover, then tap and select another mailbox.

- To undo your action, quickly swipe left with your three fingers.

Keep Deleted Emails

Deleted emails can stay in the Trash folder for up to a certain number of days. To choose the days count,

- Press **Mail** in the Settings app, select **Accounts** and tap your email account.

- Scroll to **Advanced** and select **Mail,** then tap **Advanced.**

- Press **Remove** and choose your day count.

Archive Emails

Follow the steps below to create an Archive mailbox for storing emails you do not want at the time.

- Press **Mail** in the Settings app, select **Accounts** and tap your email account.

- Scroll to **Advanced** and select **Mail,** then tap **Advanced.**

- Now change the destination mailbox for all your discarded emails to the **Archive Mailbox.**

- When next you delete an item, it will be automatically stored in the Archive folder. But if you still wish to permanently delete the email and not archive it, touch the ⬚ icon and hold until you see a menu and then select **Trash Message.**

Work with Attachments

- To save a video or photo attachment, press the item and hold until you see a menu, then select **Add to Photos.**

- To preview an attachment, press the attachment and hold until you see a list of actions on your screen.

- To view the attachment with a different app, press the attachment, and hold until you see a menu, tap ⬆ and choose the app you want to use.

View Emails with Attachments

To see all your emails that contain attachments,

- Open a mailbox in **Mails,** then tap ⊜ to enable filtering.

- Select **'Filtered By,'** then turn on the **'Only Mail with Attachments'** option.

Print an Email or Attachment

- Open the email you want to print, tap and select **Print.**

- Open an attachment or picture in an email, tap and select **Print.**

Chapter 21: Music App

The Music app on the iPhone 12 allows you to listen to music stored on your device and music streamed over the internet. There are several ways to get music on your iPhone: Subscribe to Apple Music, Purchase music from the iTunes store, Participate in Family Sharing, and Listen to Apple Music Radio.

Browse and Play Music on iPhone 12

- Click the **Library** tab in the Music app, then select a category. Tab **Downloaded** to show only the music stored on your device.
- Click the music of your choice, then click **Play.** You may also tap **Shuffle** to play the music in your playlist or album at random.
- Another way to play music is to touch and hold the album art, then select **Play.**

Sort Your Music

Sort your music according to your desired category:

- Click the **Library** tab in the Music app, then select a category like Music Videos or Songs.
- Press **Sort** and choose a method for sorting.

Play Music Shared on a Nearby Computer

A computer on your network can share music with other devices through Home Sharing. This option allows you to stream music from the computer to your iPhone.

- Press **Music** in the Settings app, tap **Sign In** under **Home Sharing.**
- Then sign in using your Apple ID.

- Return to the Music app and click the **Library** tab.

- Select **'Home Sharing'** and then choose a shared library.

See Song Details and Adjust Volume

On the Now Playing screen, you will find options for accessing and controlling music.

- Use the volume keys on your device to control media volume or drag the volume slider in the 'Now Playing' screen.

- To see details of a song, press the name of the artist underneath the song title, then choose to go to the playlist, album, or artist.

- Drag the playhead to scrub to any part of the song.

Stream Music to Bluetooth Device

- Play a song in the Music app, and tap the song at the bottom of your screen.

- Then tap to select a Bluetooth device.

Queue Up Your Music

When you play a song, the AutoPlay feature of the Music app will find similar songs and add them to the Up Next queue. Open the Queue to see all the songs that will play next, songs you played recently, and the song that is currently playing.

- Play a song in the Music app, then tap the song at the bottom of your screen.

- Tap at the bottom right side of your screen to see the 'Playing Next' queue.

- Drag the ░░ icon beside a song to move the song up or down the list.

- Click a song to begin playing it and the songs following it.

- Tap ⣍ to hide the queue.

- The Autoplay feature studies the music you play, then add similar songs to the end of the queue. Tap the ∞ icon at the top right side of your screen to disable **Autoplay.**

Note: AutoPlay is only available to Apple Music subscribers.

Choose What You Want to Play Next

To add video and music to the queue,

- Search for the song or the video in the Music app, touch and hold it, then tap the **'Play Next'** to play the music when the current one ends, or select **Play Last** to add the music to the end of the queue.

Subscribe to Apple Music

Apple Music allows you to enjoy millions of songs without interruption from ads. You can design your playlist, listen to music online and offline, see what your friends are playing, and lots more. If you are yet to subscribe, follow the steps below:

- Tap **Music** in Settings, and tap the **'Start Free Trial'** option.
- Turn on the **'Show Apple Music'** switch to see the subscription features.

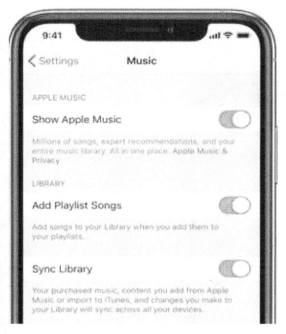

Manage Your Apple Music Subscription

To change or cancel your Apple Music subscription plan,

- Click the **Listen Now** tab in the Music app, and click your profile image. Then select **Manage Subscription** and cancel or change.

Create Your Playlist

- Click the **Library** tab in the Music app, and select **Playlists.**
- Click on **New Playlist,** choose a name for the playlist, then click on **Add Music.**
- Go through your music list and select all the music you want to add to the playlist, then tap **Done.**
- Another way to add music to a playlist is to touch the music you want to add and hold on until you see a menu, then tap the '**Add to Playlist'** option and choose a playlist or click **New Playlist** to create a different playlist.

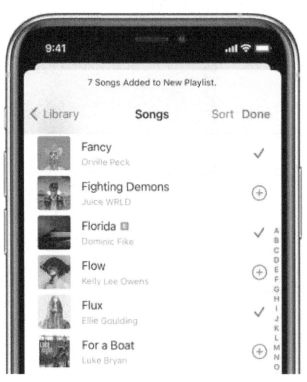

Edit a Playlist

- Open the playlist, press ● ● ● , and then tap **Edit.**

- Click on **Add Music** to add more songs to the playlist.

- Tap ⊖ beside a song to delete the song, then tap **Delete** - this will only delete the song from that playlist.

- Drag the hamburger ☰ icon beside a song to reorder the arrangement of the songs in the playlist.

Delete a Playlist

You can delete a playlist in two ways:

1. Touch and hold the playlist, then tap the **'Delete from Library'** option.

2. Open the playlist, press ● ● ● , and then tap **Delete from Library.**

Play Music from Apple Music

Follow the steps below to play music from your Apple Music subscription

- Click the **Listen Now** tab in the Music app, & click an album/ playlist.

- Then click **Play** or press **Shuffle** to shuffle your playlist or album.

- Another way to play music is to touch and hold the album or playlist, then select **Play.**

Automatically Download Music to your iPhone

When you add songs from Apple Music to your playlist, the songs are not downloaded automatically. To set up automatic download,

- Press **Music** in the Settings app, then turn on the '**Automatic Download**' switch.
- To manually download songs from Apple Music to your device, first add the songs to a playlist, then tap the ⛅ icon at the top.
- To see the download progress, click the **Library** tab, select **Downloaded Music** and click on **Downloading.**

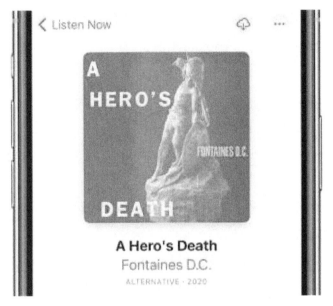

A Hero's Death
Fontaines D.C.
ALTERNATIVE · 2020

Note that you must turn on **Sync Library** before you can download music from Apple Music to your Library.

- Tap **Music** in the Settings app, then turn on the '**Sync Library**' switch.

Free Up Music Storage

When in need of storage space, your device can automatically delete any music you downloaded but haven't played in a while.

- Press **Music** in Settings, then click on **Optimize Storage.**

- Turn the switch to the **'On'** position, then choose the amount of storage space that music on your phone can take up before the device should remove your downloaded musical content.
- Once you hit the limit that you set, the device will automatically delete any downloaded songs you haven't played in a while.

Manually Delete Downloaded Music and Videos

Asides from the automatic removal of music you haven't played in a while, you can manually delete videos and music stored on your device.

- Touch and hold the item (music video, songs, playlist, TV show, movie, or album) that you downloaded, select **Remove** and tap **Remove Downloads.**
- The content will be removed from the iPhone but not the iCloud Music Library.

Delete Downloaded Songs from an Artist

123

- Tap **Music** in the Settings app, then click on **Downloaded Music.**

- Click **Edit** and press the ⊖ icon beside the artists whose music you wish to delete.

Inform Apple Music what You Love

This will help Apple Music to recommend songs and content you like.

Do any of the following:

- Touch and hold a song, playlist, or album, then press **Love** to get other similar recommendations or press **Suggest Less like This** to dislike the song.

- While on the Now Playing screen, tap ● ● ● , then press **Love** to get other similar recommendations, or press **Suggest Less like This.**

Tell Music to Ignore Your Listening Habits

Tell Apple Music not to use your listening habits in recommending music to you.

- Tap **Music** in the Settings app, then turn off the '**Use Listening History**' switch.

Rate Music in Your Library

- Tap **Music** in the Settings app, then turn on the '**Show Star Ratings**' switch.

- Go to the song you want to rate, touch, and hold the song, then select '**Rate Song**' and choose your rating.

Listen to Apple Music Radio

- Press the **Radio** tab in the Music app, then choose a radio station.

Create Apple Music Profile

As an Apple Music subscriber, you can follow your friends to see the music they are listening to. Your friends who follow you will also be able to see the music you listen to. To enjoy this service, you need to create a profile.

- Click the **Listen Now** tab in the Music app, & tap your profile image. Then press **Start Sharing with Friends** to begin.
- Press **'View Profile'** at the upper part of your screen to view your Apple music profile.

Follow or Unfollow your Friends

You can follow in two ways:

1. Go to the bottom of the profile page, tap the **'Follow More Friends'** option, and then tap the **'Follow'** button by the side of the people you want to follow.

2. Or touch and hold a friend's profile picture on the Profile page, then tap **Follow.**

- To unfollow, touch and hold a friend's profile picture on the Profile page, then select **Unfollow.**

Respond to Follow Requests

Let everyone follow you or choose people that can follow you. If you choose people that can follow you, you will always receive a Follow Request before someone can view your profile or music list.

- Click the **Listen Now** tab in the Music app, & tap your profile image.

- Click on **View Profile** and tap **Edit.**

- Then click on '**People You Approve'** to choose people that can follow you.

- Click **Follow Requests** to view all your requests, then accept or decline as you wish.

Block Followers

- Touch and hold a friend's profile picture on the Profile page, then select **Block.**

Share Music with Followers

Your followers can see all your playlists. To specify some playlists that should not be seen by your followers,

- Click the **Listen Now** tab in the Music app, & tap your profile image. Press **View Profile** and tap **Edit.**

- Then turn off all the playlists you don't want to share.

Set Music Equalizer on your iPhone

EQ allows you to adjust the sound frequencies in the songs or audio you play so they sound different from the original album.

- Press **Music** in the Settings app, then tap the '**EQ'** option under **Playback.**

- Now select an equalizer from the options on your screen.

- Tap **Off** to switch off the equalizer.

Choose Cellular Data Options for Music

Choose your preferred option for using your cellular data to play music.

- Tap **Music** in the Settings app, select the '**Cellular Data**' option, and then turn **Streaming** off or on, allow music download over cellular or Choose High-Quality Streaming.

Sound Check on iPhone

This feature equalizes the volume of all the music you downloaded, making sure that they are not too loud.

- Press **Music** in the Settings app, then turn on the '**Sound Check**' switch.

Watch YouTube in 4K

iOS 14 supports Google VP9 codec, which allows you to watch YouTube videos in 4k.

- Start a YouTube video, then bring up the menu option and choose the '**2160P**' option to switch to 4k video.

Chapter 22: Phone App

Answer Incoming Call

- Tap  to answer a call and ⬤ to end the call.
- Press the Side button or any of the volume buttons to silence an incoming call you do not want to answer.
- If the call comes while your screen is locked, you may drag the slider to answer the call.
- Tap **Keypad** to dial a number while on a call.
- Tap **Mute** to stop the other party from hearing you.
- Touch and hold **'Mute'** to place the caller on hold.

- Press **Audio** to go hands-free.
- Tap **FaceTime** to switch to FaceTime call.

Announce Incoming Calls

Would you like your iPhone to announce all calls you receive or only calls that come in when driving and connected to headphones or Bluetooth?

- Press **Phone** in the Settings app, tap the **'Announce Calls'** option, and choose an appropriate response.

Decline a Call

When you decline a call, the call will be sent automatically to voicemail.

- Tap or press the Side button twice in quick successions to decline a call.

- To get more options, swipe down on the call banner, then tap **Remind Me** to set a reminder for that call.

- To decline with a message, tap **Message,** and tap **Custom** to enter a message. You may also choose from the default response.

Create Your Default Replies

You can decline a call with a message, either a custom message or default replies available on your iPhone. Default replies are quicker ways to end a call. To edit the default replies,

- Tap **Phone** in the Settings app, then tap **'Respond with Text.'**

- Tap any of the messages on your screen and enter a new text.

Make a Call

- Open the Phone app and click the **Keypad** tab at the bottom.

- If you have double SIMs on your iPhone, tap the line at the top of your screen to select a different line for making a call.

- To redial the last number you called, tap , and then tap again to call the number.

- To paste a number you copied, click on the phone number field and then click **Paste.**

- Or manually enter the number you want to call and then tap

Redial or Return a Recent Call

- Open the Phone app, click the **'Recents'** tab**,** then click on a call to redial. To see more details about the call, tap .

Change Your Outgoing Call Settings

- Tap **Phone** in the Settings app, then turn the **'Show My Caller ID'** switch on or off. Turn it off if you want to hide your number when making a call.

- Turn on the **'Dial Assist for International Calls'** switch to instruct the iPhone to automatically add the right local or international prefix when you call your contacts.

Make Emergency Call

The Emergency SOS on iPhone allows you to easily and quickly reach out for help as well as alert your emergency contacts.

- While your iPhone is locked, tap **Emergency** on the passcode screen.

- Then dial the emergency number for your country & tap .

Use Emergency SOS

This applies to all countries except India.

- Touch and hold any of the volume buttons and the side button until you see the Emergency SOS slider, and the iPhone plays a warning sound and begins a countdown. Release the button once iPhone calls emergency services.

- At the end of the emergency call, your device will alert your emergency contacts and send them your current location.

You can also tap the side button five times to start Emergency SOS. However, this setting is not turned on automatically.

- Tap **Emergency SOS** in the Settings app, then turn on the '**Call with Side Button'** switch.

For users in India,

- Tap the side button three times to use Emergency SOS.

Change Your Emergency SOS Settings

- Tap **Emergency SOS** in the Settings app, then turn on the '**Auto Call'** switch to instruct the iPhone to call emergency services in your region when you start Emergency SOS.

- Turn the '**Countdown Sound'** switch off or on. With the switch on, your device will play a warning sound even if you turned on DND or silent mode.

- To manage your emergency contacts, click on **Edit Emergency Contacts in Health.** To add new emergency contacts, click on **Set Up Emergency Contacts in Health.**

Use Another App while on a Call

To use other apps while answering or making a call,

- Swipe up from the bottom end of your screen to go home, then open an app to use it alongside the call.

- Tap at the top of your screen to expand the call screen.

Start a Conference Call

iPhone permits you to have up to five people on a call using GSM service. This service is not available on Wi-Fi or VoLTE calling.

- After you have answered or initiated the first call, tap **Add Call** to call a different party. Once the other party answers the call, tap **Merge Calls** to join both calls. Follow this step to add all participants.

- To remove one person from the call, tap next to the person and then choose **End.**

- If you have an incoming call and want to add the caller to the conference call, tap **Hold Call + Answer,** then click on **Merge Calls.**

- To speak privately with someone from the conference call, tap next to the person, and tap **Private.** Tap **Merge Calls** to join the conference call again.

Set Up Voicemail

- Open the Phone app and click on the **Voicemail** tab at the bottom.

- Click on **Set Up Now,** and enter your preferred password.

- Then select a greeting, either Default or Custom. Custom will require you to record a new greeting.

Set Up Wi-Fi Calling

Asides from your cellular network, you can also receive and make calls through a Wi-Fi connection.

- Tap **Cellular** in the Settings app, then choose a line for Wi-Fi calling.
- Click on **Wi-Fi Calling,** and then turn on the '**Wi-Fi Calling on This iPhone'** switch. Finally, set up an address for emergency services.

Call Forwarding

Call Forwarding redirects all your incoming calls to a different number.

- Tap **Phone** in the Settings app, then click on **Call Forwarding.**
- Turn on the '**Call Forwarding'** switch.
- Click on **Forward To** and enter a different number for redirecting your calls. Use the back button to confirm your changes.
- Turn off the '**Call Forwarding'** switch if you no longer want the service.

Call Waiting

If you do not turn on Call Waiting, any new calls that come in while you are on a call will go straight to voicemail. To turn on call waiting,

- Tap **Phone** in the Settings app, then click on **Call Waiting.**
- Then turn on the '**Call Waiting'** switch.

Block Unwanted Callers

Block certain people from being able to reach you via voice calls, messages and even FaceTime calls.

- Open the Phone app and click either the **Voicemail, Favorite** or **Recents** tab.

- Tap the (i) icon next to the contact or number you wish to block, then move down and tap the '**Block this Caller**' option.

- You may also click the **Contacts** tab, tap a contact, and tap the '**Block this Caller**' option.

Manage Blocked Contacts

To see a list of all your blocked contacts as well as to unblock a contact,

- Tap **Phone** in the Settings app and press **Blocked Contacts.**

- Then click **Edit** to adjust the list.

To view your blocked contacts or unblock a contact,

- Go to Settings, tap **Phone,** and click **Blocked Contacts.**

- Tap **Edit** to modify.

Send Spam Calls to Voicemail

Your phone carrier has a way of identifying spam/ scam calls and can send such calls to voicemail if you turn on the option.

- Tap **Phone** in the Settings app, and then click '**Silence Unknown Callers**' if you do not want to be notified of incoming calls from people that are not on your contacts and are not numbers you dialed recently.

- To block spam calls, tap **Call Blocking & Identification** and then turn on the '**Silence Junk Callers**' to send the numbers identified as fraud or potential scam to voicemail.

Chapter 23: Contact App

Create a New Contact

- Open the Contacts app, click the ╋ sign and fill in the details of the new contact.

Share a Contact

- Tap a contact in the Contacts app and select **Share Contact.**
- Then choose the sharing method.

Quickly Reach a Contact

You can reach a contact right from the Contacts app.

- Tap a contact in the Contacts app and then tap **Phone** to call, tap **Message** to send a message, tap **FaceTime** to switch to FaceTime call, tap **Pay** to send or request money, and more.

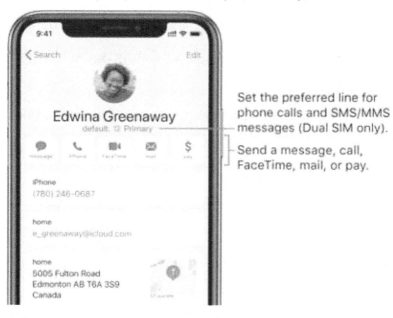

Set the preferred line for phone calls and SMS/MMS messages (Dual SIM only).

Send a message, call, FaceTime, mail, or pay.

Delete a Contact

- Click on the contact and tap **Edit** at the top.

- Then click on **Delete Contact.**

Assign Photo to a Contact

- Click on the contact and tap **Edit** at the top.

- Then click on **Add Photo** and choose a photo for the contact.

- Tap **Done** to save.

Add Your Contact Info

iPhone takes the details you inputted in your Apple ID to create your contact card. This contact card is known as **My Card.** You may still be required to provide other missing information on My Card.

- Open the Contacts app on your device, then tap **My Card** at the top of your screen.

- Tap **Edit** and enter all the required details.

- If you can't find any card, press ✛ , and then enter your details.

- Once done, go to the Settings app, click **Contacts,** tap **My Info,** then click on your name in the list.

- Tap **Siri & Search** in the Settings app, select **My Information,** then click on your name in the list.

To edit your details in *My Card,*

- Tap **My Card** at the top of the Contact apps, then click **Edit.**

Set up Your Medical ID

Include your health details like your age, medical condition, and all in the Medical ID, which is helpful in emergency cases.

- Tap **My Card** at the top of the Contact app, then click **Edit.**

- Click **Create Medical ID** to fill in your details for the first time or tap **Edit Medical ID** to update your details.

Import Contacts

To import contacts from a SIM card,

- Tap **Contacts** in the Settings app, then click **Import SIM Contacts.**

To import from a vCard,

- Click on the .vcf attachment contained in the message or email.

Add a Contact from a Directory

- Open the Contacts app and click on **Groups.**

- Then click on the directory you want to search: CardDAV, LDAP, or GAL. Tap **Done** and enter your search.

- Click on the name of the person to save their details.

Show or Hide a Group

- Open the Contacts app and click on **Groups.**

- Then choose the groups you want to hide or show.

- You will only see this button if you have multiple sources of contact.

Add a Recent Caller to Contacts

- Open the Phone app and click the **Recents** tab.

- Tap the ⓘ icon next to a number, and choose '**Add to Existing Contact'** or '**Create New Contact'** for a new contact.

Link Contacts

The iPhone should automatically link two entries for the same person. However, if you wish to do this manually,

- Open one of the contacts and click **Edit.**

- Click on **Link Contacts** and select the second entry, and then tap **Link.**

Chapter 24: Browse the Web Using Safari

Safari, Apple's web browser, continues to get better and faster with lots of updates and add-ons. The browser includes a smart search bar that you can use to search through your browsing history and saved bookmarks.

Choose a Default Search Engine in Safari

To choose a default search engine for all your searches on Safari,

- Tap **Safari** in the Settings app, then click on **Search Engine** and choose one of the options on your screen.

Search the Web Using Smart Search Bar

The Smart Search bar combines the old address and search bars into a universal space that you can use to access your browsing history, default search provider, saved bookmarks, and even search for specific words on a web page.

- Open Safari and tab the **Smart Search Bar** at the top of the page.

- Enter a search phrase or keyword in the bar and then tap **Go** on your keyboard to view the search results.

Search Within Websites

To find a phrase or keyword within a website, use the search field at the top of the screen to enter the name of the website, followed by the keyword or phrase you want. For instance, enter 'Amazon iPhone 12' to search Amazon for iPhone 12 devices. To enable or disable this feature,

- Tap **Safari** in the Settings app, click on **Quick Website Search** and then turn on the switch.

Search a Webpage

To find a specific phrase or keyword on a page,

- Tap ⬆️ and then tap the **'Find on Page'** option.

- Enter a keyword or phrase in the search field and then click ∨ to find other instances of the term or phrase.

Navigate Websites on Safari

Tips below will guide you on navigating a website:

- Tap the top of a webpage twice to return to the top of the page for a long webpage.

- Rotate to landscape orientation to view more of a page.

- Tap ⬆️ to share a link to the page.

- Tap ↻ at the top of the page to refresh.

- Pinch closed or open to zoom.

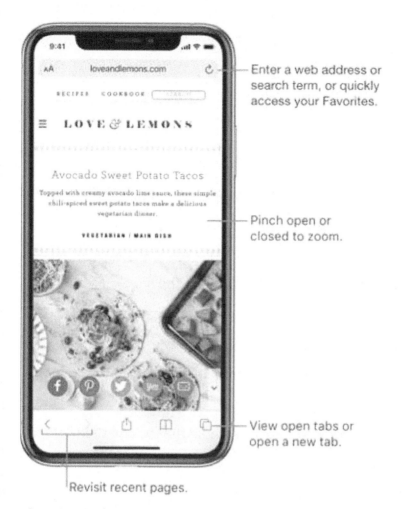

Enter a web address or search term, or quickly access your Favorites.

Pinch open or closed to zoom.

View open tabs or open a new tab.

Revisit recent pages.

Change Display, Text Size, and Website Settings

- Tap AA at the top of the webpage, then tap the large A to increase the font size or tap the small A to decrease the font size.

- To stop seeing the search field, click on **Hide Toolbar.** Click the top of your screen to return the search field.

- Click on **Request Desktop Website** to switch to the desktop version of that webpage.

- Click on **Show Reader View** to hide ads and navigation menus on that web page (if available).
- To set privacy and display controls for any time you visit this website, click on **Website Settings.**

Translate a Webpage

- Tap AA at the top of the webpage, then click ![icon] to choose the second language.

Preview Website Link

To get a quick preview of a link without visiting the page,

- Touch and hold the link, and a preview of the webpage will open.
- Click any part of the screen to exit the preview.
- Click on the link to quickly open it either in the current tab or a new tab.
- To open it in a new tab, touch and hold the link and then click on **Open in New Tab.**

Stay on Current Tab

Whenever you launch a link in a new tab, the browser switches to the new tab. To remain on the current tab,

- Tap **Safari** in the Settings app, click **Open Links,** and tap the 'In Background' option.

Browse Open Tabs

- To see all the tabs you have open, click the ![icon] button at the end of your screen.

- Swipe left on a tab to close it or tap the ✕ button at the top left side of the tab.

- To return to a tab, click the tab or click **Done** to go back to the current page you are viewing.

- To see a history of the links you opened in a tab, touch and hold either ❮ or ❯.

Reopen Recently Closed Bar

To reopen a bar that you closed recently,

- Open Safari and tab ⬜ at the bottom, then touch and hold the ✚ sign and select your choice from the list of closed tabs.

Show or Hide Tab Bar

The tab bar shows all the open tabs you have at the time.

- Tap **Safari** in the Settings app, then turn on the **'Show Tab Bar'** switch.

Bookmark Current Page

Bookmark webpages to easily revisit them in the nearest future.

- Open a URL in Safari, scroll down, touch and hold 📖, then tap **Add Bookmark.** Tap the 📖 button again to view all your bookmarks.

Add a Webpage to Your Favorite

- Open a URL in Safari, scroll down, tap ⬆, then click on **Add to Favorites.**

- Tap the 📖 button at the bottom of the page to view all your Favorites – tap **Favorites,** then click on **Edit** to delete, rename or rearrange the Favorite tabs.

Add a Website Icon to your Home Screen

If you have a website that you visit frequently, you can add an icon for that website to your home screen for easy access subsequently.

- Open a URL in Safari, scroll down, tap ⬆️, then click on **Add to Home Screen.**

Add Current Page to Your Reading List

The reading list contains articles that you may be interested in revisiting later.

- Open a URL in Safari, scroll down, tap ⬆️, then click on **Add to Reading List.**
- To add a link to the reading list without opening it, press down on the link, and then tap the '**Add to Reading List'** option.
- To view your reading list, tap 📖 and then click on 👓 .

Add a Credit Card for Purchases

Set up a credit card for your online purchases:

- Tap **Safari** in the Settings app and select **Autofill.**
- Then click on **Saved Credit Cards,** press **Add Credit Card** and then enter your card details manually or tap **Use Camera** to scan the card.

- To use the credit card details when making an online purchase, click on **AutoFill Credit Card** close to the keyboard, then enter the card's security code.

Block Pop-Ups

- Tap **Safari** in the Settings app, then turn on the **'Block Pop-Ups'** switch.

Delete Browsing History

- Tap **Safari** in the Settings app, then tap the **'Clear History and Website Data'** option.

Private Browsing

Private Browsing mode ensures that the sites you visit do not track your location, neither is the history of visited sites stored on your iPhone.

- Tap at the bottom of the Safari browser, then select **Private.**

- To return to normal view, tap again and then click on **Private.**

Stop Seeing Frequently Visited Sites

Open Safari & scroll down to view your frequently visited sites. But you can choose not to have your frequently visited sites on the Safari home page.

- Go to Settings, tap **Safari,** and disable **Frequently Visited Sites.**

View Privacy Report

The Safari app stops trackers from monitoring your online activities. The Privacy Report shows the privacy tracking objects that the browser encountered while you were surfing the current webpage.

- Open a URL in Safari, tap  at the top of the screen, then click

 **Privacy Report.**

Change Default Browser

While Safari is cool to use, you can now use a different browser as your default.

- Open **Settings**, and click on the third-party browser that you want to use as your default.

- Tap **Default Browser App,** and then choose the third party browser.

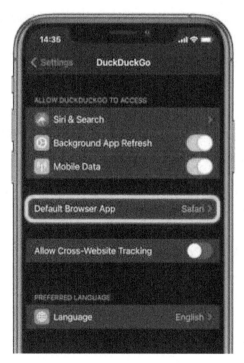

Chapter 25: Camera App

Take a Photo

- Tap the Camera icon on your home screen to launch the iPhone camera.

- To set a timing before the shutter sound goes off, click the ⌃ icon, then click ⏱.

- Click the ⚡ icon to turn Flash on or off.
- Pinch the screen to zoom in or out.

- Tap the 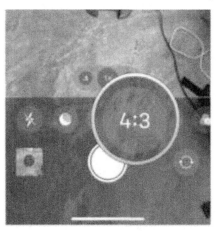 icon close to the bottom of the screen to switch between the front-facing and rear-facing cameras.

- Then tap the White shutter button or one of the volume buttons to take a picture.

Mirror Front Camera

You can take a selfie that captures the photo as if you were staring at yourself in the mirror.

- Tap **Camera** in the **Settings** app, then turn on the '**Mirror Front Camera.'**

Take a Square Photo on your iPhone

- Open the Camera app and tap the arrow at the top of your screen. Then click the **Aspect Ratio** button and choose **Square.**

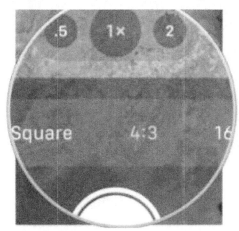

Use the Headset Remote to Take a Picture

You can also use the volume up buttons on your headsets to take a picture on your iPhone.

- Simply position your subject in the camera frame and then press the volume up button on your headset to take the photo.

Panorama Mode

This mode is best for capturing landscapes and images that may be too wide or big for your camera screen.

- Swipe to **Pano** mode and then press the Shutter button.
- Move your camera slowly while following the direction of the arrow.
- Then press the Shutter button to stop recording.

Take a Live Photo

Live Photos show the event that occurred just before and after a photo was captured.

- Swipe to the Photo mode and tap ⦿ to switch to **Live Photos.**

- Then use the shutter or volume button to take a photo.

Use Night Mode

Night Mode gives you great quality pictures in low-light conditions. You can use the Night mode on both the front and rear cameras on your iPhone 12.

- Swipe to the Photo mode, and Night Mode will automatically come on once the device identifies poor-lighting condition.

- The ◉ button at the top of your screen will turn yellow, with a number beside the button indicating the number of seconds before the camera will take the shot.

- To further customize your options, press the ◉ button, and then choose either **Max** or **Auto** timers. Whatever option you go for will apply the next time you use this mode.

- Tap the Shutter button and then hold your camera still to capture the image. Ensure to remain still while taking the photo to avoid distortion of the image. Tap the **Stop** button under the slider to stop shooting in Night mode before the timer runs out.

Take a Photo with a Filter

Add filters to your live photos:

- Swipe to either Portrait or Photo mode, press , and then press
  . The filters will show under the viewer. Click on a filter to use
  it on your photo.

Take Burst Shots

Take several high-speed images within a short time, and then make your choice from the collection. Use with either the front or rear cameras.

- Pull the shutter button to your left and hold the button in place to take the burst shots. Release the button to stop the burst shots.

- Tap the image thumbnail at the bottom of your screen to view all the images taken. To choose the images you want to keep, tap **Select.** Press the circle by the side of the images you want to save, and then tap **Done.** You will find Gray dots under the thumbnails suggesting the images that you should keep.

- If you wish to delete the burst shots, press the thumbnail and then press the  button.

Use Volume Up Button to Take Burst Shots

Asides from swiping and holding the shutter button, holding the volume up button will also take the burst shots.

- Tap **Camera** in the Settings app and then turn on the '**Use Volume up for Burst'** switch.

Take Videos

- Swipe to Video mode and then press either the volume or record button to start recording.

- While video recording, press the white shutter button close to the end of the screen to take a still picture.

- Pinch closed or open to zoom. To get an accurate zoom, press and hold 1x, and then pull the slider to the left.

- Press either the volume or record button to stop recording.

Change Frame Rate

To change the video frame rate and resolution settings,

- Tap **Camera** in the Settings app, press **Record Video,** and make the necessary changes.

Turn off Stereo Sound

The iPhone 12 uses several microphones to give users the best stereo sound for their video recordings. To turn off the stereo recording,

- Tap **Camera** in the Settings app, then turn off the '**Record Stereo Sound'** option.

Turn off HDR Recording

iPhone 12 models record videos in HDR, which you can share with other Apple devices using iPadOS 13.4, macOS 10.15.4, iOS 13.4, or later. To disable HDR recording,

- Tap **Camera** in the Settings app, tap **Record Video,** and then turn off the '**HDR Video'** option.

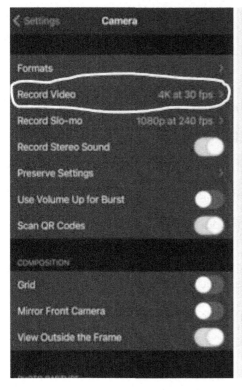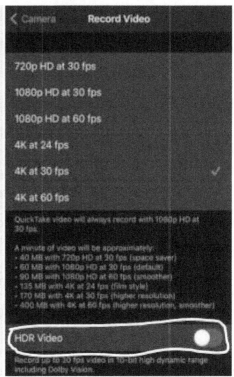

Capture a Time-Lapse Video

Record a video at different intervals and then combine them to create a time-lapse video of an action over time, e.g., a setting sun. Use a tripod to get the best and stable video.

- Swipe to **Time-Lapse** mode and position your device properly.
- Then press the volume or shutter button to start or stop the recording.

Record Quick Take Video

To take a video without swiping to the video mode,

- Touch and hold the shutter button in the Photo mode to start the video.

154

- Move the shutter button to your right and release it over the lock (Record button) to do a hands-free recording.
- With the buttons locked, press the shutter button to capture a still photo during the recording. Press the Record button to stop the record.

Record Slow-mo Video

Record your video as normal, and then play it back in slow motion.

- Swipe to **Slow-mo** mode, and press the  button to record with the front camera if you like.
- Press the volume or shutter button to start or stop the recording.
- To have only a part of the video playback in slow-motion while the rest continue at the regular speed, click the video thumbnail at the bottom and select **Edit.** Then pull the vertical bars underneath the frame viewer to choose the sections that should playback in slow motion.

Portrait Mode

Portrait mode applies studio-quality lighting effects to your images. This mode pays focus on the subject and blurs the background.

- Swipe to **Portrait** mode and then follow the suggestions on your screen to fit the subject into the yellow portrait box.

- To make the background more or less blurry, tap 𝑓 at the top right side of your screen, then pull the slider to the left or the right until you get your desired background.

- Drag the icon on your screen to choose a lighting effect – play around with the different effects until you see one you like, then tap the shutter button to take the picture.

Remove Portrait Mode Effect

To remove the Portrait mode effect in your Portrait mode photos,

- Open the Portrait image in the Photo app, and tap **Edit.**
- Then press **Portrait** at the top to turn it on or off.

Preserve Camera Settings

Save the last camera settings you used, so they do not reset the next time you open the Camera app – settings like Live Photo, filter, depth, lighting, and camera mode.

- Tap **Camera** in the Settings app and click on **Preserve Settings.**
- Then turn on the switch for the different settings you want to preserve.

Adjust Auto FPS Settings

In a bid to improve the quality of your videos in low-light conditions, the iPhone will automatically reduce the frame rate to 24 fps. To choose when this setting should apply,

- Tap **Camera** in the Settings app and click on **Record Video.**
- Tap **Auto FPS,** and then choose whether the FPS settings should apply to just the 30fps videos or both the 30 and 60 fps videos.

Turn off Prioritize Faster Shooting

This setting changes the way the iPhone processes images so that you can get faster shooting when you rapidly press the shutter button. It is turned on by default. To turn it off,

- Tap **Camera** in the Settings app and then turn off the '**Prioritize Faster Shooting'** option.

Disable Scene Detection

The iPhone 12 camera lens automatically identifies objects in different scenes and then improves them. It is turned on by default. To turn scene detection off,

- Tap **Camera** in the Settings app and then turn off the **'Scene Detection'** option.

Turn off Lens Correction

Lens correction adjusts the images taken with the ultra-wide camera or the front camera to give it a more natural look. It is turned on by default. To turn lens correction off,

- Tap **Camera** in the Settings app and then turn off the **'Lens Correction'** option.

Turn Off Automatic HDR

HDR (High Dynamic Range) helps put true-to-life color and contrast in your video, thereby getting great shots in high-contrast conditions. This setting is turned on by default. To disable,

- Tap **Camera** in the Settings app and then turn off the **'Smart HDR'** option.

- With this option disabled, you can manually control HDR in your videos by tapping **HDR** at the top of your screen to turn it off or on.

Use the Camera to Read a QR Code

- Swipe to Photo mode and position the camera lens over the code.

- Then tap the notification from the code to launch the app or website.

Chapter 26: Photos App

Every photo and video you have on your device is stored in the Photos app, organized into months, days, years, and All Photos.

Tap to share, play movie, and see location on a map.

Tap to view full screen.

- Tap the **Library** tab to see all your videos and photos organized by months, days, and years.
- Tap the **For You** tab to view a personalized feed showing your shared albums, memories, and featured photos.
- Tap the **Search** tab to search for your photos or videos by captions, location, date, etc.

- Tap the **Albums** tab to see all the albums you created or shared.

View Individual Photos

To see individual photos, click the **All Photos** or the **Library** tabs.

- Press an image to view it on full screen
- Pinch out or double-tap your screen to zoom in. Pinch in or double-tap your screen to zoom out.
- Tap ⬆️ to share the image or tap ♡ to Favorite the image.
- Swipe up on the image to view or add captions in the text field close to the bottom of your screen.
- Tap ‹ to go back to all Photos.

Play a Live Photo

Live Photos ◎ show the event that occurred just before and after a photo was captured – in a movie form. To play

- Tap the Live Photo to open it, then press and hold the image to watch it play.

See your Burst Shot Images

After taking your Burst Shots, you can choose to save some and delete the rest.

- Open any of the Burst photos on your device and tap **Select.**
- Go through the images in the collection to find the ones you want to save separately.
- To save images from the collection, touch the images to select them, then click **Done.**

- Tap the '**Keep Everything**' option to save the images separately and still keep the Burst or tap the '**Keep Only (number) Favorites**' option to delete the images you didn't select.

Play a Video

- Open Photos and click on the **Library** tab.

- Click on a video to play it in full screen – the video will play without sound.

- Press the player controls underneath the video to unmute, mute, pause, or play. Tap your screen to make the controls invisible.

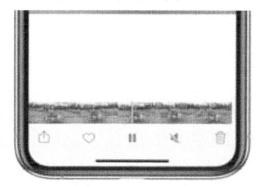

- Tap your screen twice to move between full screen and 'fit-to-screen.'

Play & Customize a Slideshow

A slideshow collects all your pictures, formats them, and then add music.

- Open Photos and click on the **Library** tab.

- Tap **Days** or **All Photos** to view all your photos, then tap **Select** to choose the images for the slideshow.

- Select the images by tapping them, then tap ⬆️.

- Select **Slideshow** from the options, tap your screen, and then tap **Options** to edit the slideshow.

Show Your Photos on Apple TV/ an AirPlay 2-Enabled TV

- Select the images by tapping them, then tap ⬆️.

- Press **AirPlay** and then select the smart TV or Apple TV as the playback destination.

- Enter your device passcode if you see a prompt on your TV screen asking for an AirPlay passcode.

Hide Photos and Videos

To hide a video or photos from showing in the Library tab,

- Open the photo or video, tap ⬆️, and then select **Hide.**

- Go to the **Hidden** album to find all the hidden photos and videos.

To hide the Hidden Album from showing in **Albums,**

- Tap **Photos** in the Settings app and then turn off the **'Hidden Album'** switch.

Delete Photos and Videos

- Open the photo or video, and tap 🗑️.

- You will find your deleted videos and photos in the **Recently Deleted** album for up to 30 days before removing them from the device.

Permanently Delete or Recover Deleted Photos

- Press the **Albums** tab, scroll to **Utilities** and select **Recently Deleted.**

- Tap **'Select'** and click on all the videos and photos you want.

- Then tap **Delete** or **Recover.**

Adjust Color and Light in Your Photos or Videos

- Open the video or photo you want to edit, then tap **Edit.**

- Swipe left under the image or video to see different editing buttons. Click on a button, and then drag the slider until you get the desired effect.

- Tap the ⬤ button to add effects to your videos or photos automatically.

- Tap the effect button to compare the before and after versions of the picture or video.

- Tap **Done** if satisfied with your work, or tap **Cancel** to discard.

Crop or Rotate a Photo or Video

- Open the video or photo you want to edit, then tap **Edit.**

- Tap the 🔲 icon and then do any of the following:

- Drag the rectangle corners to manually crop the images or tap the

  🔲 icon to crop to a standard preset ratio.

- Tap 🔲 to rotate the content or tap ◣◢ to flip it horizontally.

- Tap **Done** if satisfied with your work, or tap **Cancel** to discard.

Straighten and Adjust Perspective

- Open the video or photo you want to edit, then tap **Edit.**

- Tap ⬚ and then use one of the effect buttons to straighten the image as well as adjust the horizontal or vertical perspective.

- Then drag the slider until you get the desired effect.

Drag to tilt or straighten.

- The yellow outline around the buttons shows the level of adjustment made for each effect to give you an idea of the effect that was reduced or increased. Click on the button to switch between the original and edited effects.

- Tap **Done** if satisfied with your work, or tap **Cancel** to discard.

Apply Filter Effects

- Open the video or photo you want to edit, then tap **Edit.**

- Tap the button and then choose one of the effects close to the bottom of the screen.

- Tap the filter you want, then pull the slider until you get the effect you desire.

- Touch the image to switch between the original and edited effects.

- Tap **Done** if satisfied with your work, or tap **Cancel** to discard.

Revert to Original Version of a Picture or Video

After you save the changes to your edited video or photo, you can still return the image to its original form.

- Open the video or photo you edited, then tap **Edit.**

- Press **Revert** and then select the **'Revert to Original'** option.

Mark up a Photo

Use Markup to draw and write, add signature, crop, rotate, and add shapes to your image.

- Open the photo you want to edit, then tap **Edit.**

- Touch the button and select **Markup** .

- Then draw or color the images using the drawing tools on your screen. Tap the  button to add your signature, text, or shape to the image.

Trim a Video

Reduce the duration of a video

- Open the video you want to edit, then tap **Edit.**

- Drag the end of the frame viewer to edit the video's start and end points, then tap **Done.**

- If you want to save both the new video and the original video, click on the '**Save Video as New Clip'** option. If you prefer to keep just the edited video, tap **Save Video.**

Edit a Live Photo

- Open the Live Photo you want to edit, then tap **Edit.**

- Tap ⊚ close to the bottom of your screen and then drag the ends of the frame viewer to trim the live photo.

- Tap **Live** at the top-center side of your screen to turn a Live Photo into a Still Photo. Tap the button again to revert.

- To choose an image in the Live Photo that should serve as the key photo, move the white frame on the frame viewer to the desired image, press **Make Key Photo,** and then press **Done.**

- Tap  to mute the photo. Tap it again to unmute.

Add Effects to Live Photos

Edit your Live Photos to be as fun as you want them.

- Open a Live Photo, and then swipe up to show all the effects.

- Now choose an effect you want to use in your video – choose **Loop** to continuously repeat actions in the video, choose **Bounce** to rewind the actions forward and backward, or choose **Long Exposure** to blur motion in the video and give it a DSLR-like long exposure effect.

Edit Portrait Images

Portrait mode applies studio-quality lighting effects to your images. This mode pays focus on the subject and blurs the background.

- Open a photo you took in Portrait mode and then tap **Edit.**

- To make the background more or less blurry, tap ***f*** at the top right side of your screen. Then pull the slider to the left and the right until you get your desired background.

- Drag the ⬡ icon on your screen to choose a lighting effect – play around with the different effects until you see one you like.

- Tap **Done** to save the editing.

- Tap **Portrait** at the upper side of your screen to remove the Portrait effect from that image.

- To undo the changes you made to the photo, tap **Edit,** and select **Revert.** This will return the image to its original form.

Organize Photos in Albums

Albums make your Photo app look neat and arranged. Go to the Album tab to see the albums you created, the ones created automatically, and the ones you shared. See below how to create an album.

- Open the **Albums** tab and tap ┼ .
- Tap an option on the next screen: **New Shared Album** or **New Album.**
- Give your album a name and tap **Save.**
- Select the photos that should go into the album and then tap **Done.**

Add Pictures and Videos to an Album

After you create your album, you can always manually add new photos and videos.

- Go to the **Library** tab in Photos and tap **Select.**
- Select the videos and photos that should go into the album and then tap ⬆️ .
- Swipe up and then click on **Add to Album.**
- Now choose an album on your screen.

Delete Videos and Pictures from an Album

- Go to the desired album and press the video or photo you want to remove, then tap 🗑️ to remove the photo from just the album or across all your connected devices.

Delete or Rearrange Existing Albums

- Go to the **Album** tab and tap **See All.**

- Tap **Edit,** then tap ⊖ beside an album to delete it.

- To rearrange albums in the folder, tap and hold the thumbnail for one album and pull it to a different position.

- To rename an album, tap the name and set a new name.

- Tap **Done** to finish.

Sort Pictures in Albums

Sort your videos and images by oldest to newest or newest to oldest.

- Go to the **Album** tab in Photos and choose an album.

- Press the ⋯ icon and then tap **Sort.**

Filter Images and Videos in Albums

Filter content of an album by videos, pictures, edited, and favorites.

- Go to the **Album** tab in Photos and choose an album.

- Press the ⋯ icon and then tap **Filter.**

- Choose the filter option and tap **Done.**

- To remove the filter from that album, open the album, tap ☰ , tap the '**All Items'** option and then tap **Done.**

Share or Save a Shared Image or Video

When you receive videos and images from others, you can share or save them with the steps below:

- If received via mail, click on the item to download it, then tap ⬆.

Or you may tap and hold the attachment and then choose the option to share or save.

- If received via text message, click on the video or image, tap ⬆️, and then choose to share or save.

- If using an iCloud link, click on the link to see the collections, tap the collection you want to share, tap ⚫ and then click on **Share.**

Share Your Photos

To share your photos from the Photos app,

- Open the item you want, tap ⬆️ and select a method to send the photo to your receiver.

Chapter 27: The Health App

The Health app  is equipped to track the flights of stairs you climb every day as well as your daily footsteps. It also allows you to add other details like your weight, height, and so on.

Manually Update Your Health Profile

When you launch the Health app for the first time, you will need to create a health profile with your basic details like sex and date of birth. You can always update these details at a later time.

- Tap your initials or profile image at the top side of the Health app.
- Tap the **'Health Details'** option and click on **Edit.**

- Make the necessary changes and tap **Done.**

Manually Add Data to a Health Category

- Click on the **Browse** tab close to the end of your screen on the Health app.

- Then select a category or click on the search field and then enter the name of the category you want.

- Go to the data you want to update and tap ⟩.

- Press **Add Data** at the top, add your data, and tap **Done** or **Add** at the top to finish.

Collect Data from Other Sources

The Health app also collects data from sources like headphones, Apple Watch, Bluetooth devices, etc.

- When you pair your iPhone with Apple Watch, the heart rate measurement will be sent automatically from the watch to the Health App.

- When you download an app from the App Store, you can allow the app to share data with the Health app when setting up the app.

- When you connect the AirPods, EarPods, and other compatible headphones to your device, the audio levels of the headphones are sent automatically to the Health app.

View Your Health Information

The health app shows both your fitness and health details in one place. You can see how much of your fitness goals you achieved over a period, etc.

- Tap **Summary** at the bottom of the Health app, then scroll down for a summary of your data.

- For more details about a category, tap the ⟩ button beside the category.

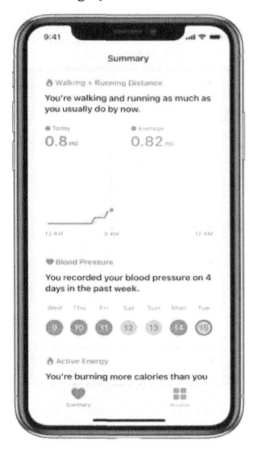

Add a Health Category to Favorites

The Summary screen of the Health app shows the health categories that you add as Favorites. To add or remove a category,

- Tap **Summary** at the bottom of the Health app, scroll to the Favorites section, and click on **Edit.**
- Select a category to add or remove it, then click on **Done.**

View Details in the Health Categories

- Tap **Browse** at the bottom of the Health app.

- Then select a category or click on the search field and enter the name of the category you want.

- The next page will show your health details for that category.

- Tap the ⟩ button to know more about a field under a category.

- Depending on the type of data, you may be able to make some changes or delete data.

- Press the tabs at the upper part of the screen to view the monthly, weekly & yearly view for that info.

- To add that field to Favorites, turn on the **'Add to Favorites'** switch. Scroll down if you do not see the option.

- Tap the '**Add Data**' option at the top right side to manually enter data.

- To delete a data in the current field, click the '**Show All Data**' menu under **Options,** swipe left on the record you wish to delete, and then tap **Delete.** To wipe all the data at once, tap **Edit** and tap **Delete All.**

- To choose a different measurement unit, click the '**Unit**' menu under **Options,** and then choose the unit of your choice.

- To see the apps and devices that you permitted to share your health record, click the '**Data Sources & Access**' menu under **Options**

Share Your Health Data

- Press your initials or profile picture at the top right side of your screen. Click on **Export All Health Data,** and select a method to share your data.

Track Your Menstrual Cycle

Enter details of your monthly cycle to receive notifications on your fertility window and possible next cycle. To start,

- Tap **Browse** at the bottom of the Health app and click on **Cycle Tracking.**

- Click on **Get Started** and follow the directions on your screen.

Log Your Cycle Information

- Tap **Browse** at the bottom of the Health app and click on **Cycle Tracking.** Then do any of the actions below:

- To log your period, select the day in the timeline on your screen.

- To enter the flow level for the period, click on **Period,** and select an option. Or, click **Add Period** at the upper part of your screen and select the days of the period days from the calendar. Click on a logged day to remove it – these are days marked with solid red circles on the timeline.

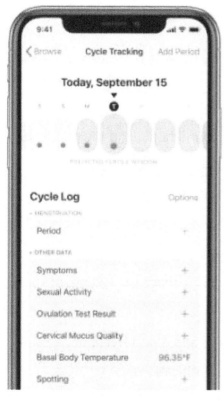

- To log spotting, choose a day on the timeline, tap **Spotting,** select the **'Had Spotting'** option, and click **Done.**
- To log your symptoms, choose a day on the timeline, click **Symptoms,** and choose all the suitable options. Tap **Done** to go to the previous screens. The purple dots on the timeline represents days with symptoms.

- To add other details like ovulation test results, click on **Options,** and select the appropriate category.

Change Fertility and Period Reminders

- Tap **Browse** at the bottom of the Health app and click on **Cycle Tracking.**
- Press **Options** and then tap an option to turn it on or off.

Collect Headphones' Audio Levels

The Health app shows the exposure levels for sounds on your headphone and Apple Watch.

- Pair a compatible headphone to your iPhone, and the headphone audio level will be sent automatically to the Health app.

See the Headphone Notifications for Loud Headphone Audio

When you stay connected to a headphone and listen to the audio for an extended period and at a volume that could harm your hearing, the iPhone will send you a notification and automatically reduce the volume of sound to protect your hearing. To receive this notification,

- Tap **Sounds & Haptics** in the Settings app, select **Headphone Safety,** and then turn on the '**Headphone Notifications'** switch.

To view a report of this notification,

- Open the Browse tab in the health screen, select **Hearing,** click on **Headphone Notifications,** and then click on the notification.

View Noise Notifications for Loud Sounds

This setting requires that you pair your Apple Watch with your iPhone as well as set up the Noise app on the iWatch. The watch will then automatically send the environmental sound levels to the Health app. The

Apple Watch will then notify the iPhone when the noise in your environment rises to a level that can damage your hearing.

- Open the **Browse** tab in the health screen, and click on **Hearing.**
- Click on **Noise Notifications** and click on a notification for more details.

View Details about Your Sound and Audio Level Exposure

- Open the **Browse** tab in the health screen, and click on **Hearing.**
- Choose an option - **Environmental Sound Levels** or **Headphone Audio Levels** – and then perform any of the actions below:
- Click on the tabs at the top of your screen to view your exposure over a period.
- Tap ⓘ to find out what the sound level classification means.
- Swipe the graph to view it in different periods.
- Scroll down to view the highlights, and tap **Show All** for a detailed view.
- If you have more than one pair of headphones, you can filter the data by the headphones. Click on **Show All Filters,** move to the end of the screen and click on the headphones.

Limit Headphone Volume

Choose a maximum limit for music and videos when using headphones to protect your hearing.

- Tap **Sounds & Haptics** in the Settings app, select **Headphone Safety.**
- Turn on the **'Reduce Loud Sounds'** switch and then choose the maximum decibel level using the slider.

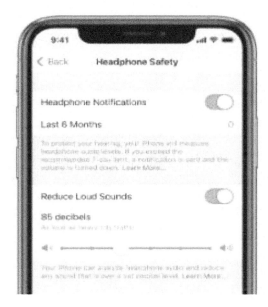

Set Up Sleep Schedule

Create a sleep schedule that includes your sleep and wake up time. You can also create different schedules for different days or periods. Each schedule allows you to choose how you want your device to wake up by selecting an alarm and other options.

- Open the **Browse** tab in the health screen, and click on **Sleep.**
- Scroll up to **Set Up Sleep** and click on **Get Started,** then follow the directions on your screen to complete.

Change Your Next Alarm

This setting allows you to change your sleep schedule for just a day – make your alarm go off later or earlier. To temporarily change your sleep schedule,

- Open the **Browse** tab in the health screen, and click on **Sleep.**
- Move down to the **'Your Schedule'** section and click on **Edit** by the side of a schedule.

- Drag the  and buttons on the circle to adjust your bedtime and wake up time.

- Turn off the **'Wake Up Alarm'** switch if desired, then adjust the sound to the appropriate level.

- Tap **Done** to save or **Cancel** to discard.

Edit Your Sleep Schedule

To change or add a new sleep schedule,

- Open the **Browse** tab in the health screen, and click on **Sleep.**

- Move down to the '**Your Schedule**' section and click on **Full Schedule & Options.**

- Click on the '**Add Schedule for Other Days**' option to add a new schedule or tap **Edit** beside a schedule to change the schedule.

- Select a day at the top of your screen to remove or add it to your schedule. The solid-color circles represent the days with schedules.

- Drag the and buttons on the circle to adjust your bedtime and wake up time.

- Adjust the **Wake Up Alarm** option as you like.

- To delete a schedule, click the **Delete Schedule** option at the bottom of the screen or tap **Cancel** at the top to discard any changes.

- Tap **Add** for new schedule or **Done** for changes made.

Change Your Sleep Goal

- Open the **Browse** tab in the health screen, and click on **Sleep.**

- Move down to the '**Your Schedule**' section and click on **Full Schedule & Options.**

- Click on **Sleep Goal** and choose a time.

- Tap **Options** to turn other options off or on.

View Your Sleep History

The sleep data will give you a clearer insight into your sleep habits.

- Open the **Browse** tab in the health screen, and click on **Sleep.**

- Press the tab at the top to see the sleep data by month or week.

- Swipe the graph from side to side to view different periods.

- Click on the '**Show More Sleep Data**' option for extensive sleep data.

- Click on the column for the present day to view details for that day.

- Press the **'Add Data'** option in the top-right to manually add sleep data.

Automatically Download your Health Records

You can view your health information/ data from supported health organizations on the Health app – information like medications, conditions, allergies, and more. This service is not available in all regions or countries. Follow the steps below to set up automatic downloads:

- Press your initials or profile image at the top right side of your screen.

- Click on the **'Health Records'** option, then tap **Get Started** to begin your first download, or click on **Add Account** to add more accounts.

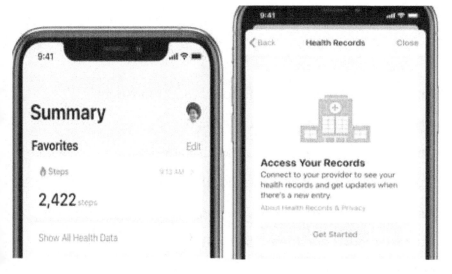

- Type in the name of the health facility that has your health records or enter the name of the state or city you live in to get a list of the health facilities nearby.

- Click on a result to open it.

- Scroll to the '**Available to Connect**' section and click **Connect to Account.**

- On the sign-in screen, you will need to enter your user name and password that you use to access the patient web portal for the health facility, then continue with the directions on your screen.

View Your Health Record

To see your health records from the different health facilities you subscribe to,

- Open the **Browse** tab in the Health app, and select a category under **Health Records.** Or, touch the search field, type the name of the data type (like Blood Pressure) or the health record category (like

Clinical Vitals). Or click on a specific health facility close to the bottom of the screen.

- Tap any field that has the ⟩ button to view more details.

Delete a Health Organization and its Record

You can remove any organization you added at any time.

- Press your initials or profile image at the top right side of your screen
- Click on the **'Health Records'** option, touch the organization you want to remove, and then click the **'Remove Account'** option.

Create or Edit Your Medical ID

Set up an emergency Medical ID with your health details like your medications, conditions, allergies, and more. During emergencies, first responders will view the information on your phone screen even when locked.

- Press your initials or profile image at the top right side of your screen
- To set up your Medical ID, click on **Get Started.** Click on **Edit** to make changes to the Medical ID.
- The **'Show When Locked'** switch is turned on by default to allow first responders to access your data in an emergency.
- Turn on the **'Share During Emergency Call'** option to share your Medical ID when you call emergency service.

First responders can access your Medical ID by swiping up on your Lock screen, click the **Emergency** option on the **Passcode** screen, and then click on **Medical ID.**

- To quickly see your Medical ID from your device's home screen, tap and hold the Health app's icon on the app library or home screen, and then tap the '**Medical ID**' option.

Chapter 28: Clock App

Use the Clock app to set alarms and view the time in different cities in the world.

View the Time in Cities Worldwide

- Click the **World Clock** tab in the Clock app and tap **Edit.**

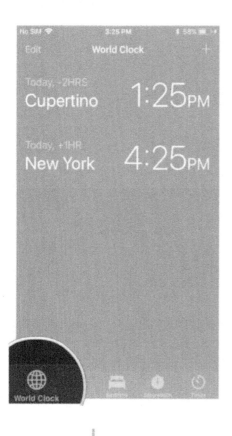 

- Tap to add a city, tap the search bar, enter the name of the city and select it from the search result.

- Tap to delete a city.

- Drag the icon beside a city to reorder the list.

188

Set an Alarm

- Click the **Alarm** tab in the Clock app and tap ✛.

- Choose the desired time, then tap **Repeat** to select the days of the week the alarm should work.

- Tap **Label** to name your alarm.

- Tap **Sound** to select vibration or sound for the alarm.

- Turn on the **'Snooze'** switch to see a snooze option when your alarm sounds.

- Tap **Save** to finish.

Edit an Alarm

- Click the **Alarm** tab in the Clock app and tap **Edit.**

- Click the alarm you want to edit, make the corrections, and tap **Save.**

Delete an Alarm

You can delete an alarm in three different ways:

- Swipe left on the alarm and tap **Delete.**
- Click the **Alarm** tab in the Clock app and tap **Edit** at the top right, then tap  beside the alarm and tap **Delete.**
- Click the **Alarm** tab in the Clock app and tap **Edit** at the top right, click the alarm, and tap **Delete Alarm.**

Set the Alarm's Volume

- Tap **Sounds and Haptics** in the Settings app.

- Scroll to the **'Ringers and Alerts'** option and move the slider right or left to set the volume.

- Turn on the **'Change with Buttons'** switch to use the Volume keys on your iPhone to change the alarm volume.

Set the Timer

- Click the **Timer** tab, set the duration for the timer, set the sound that should play when the timer ends, then click **Start**.

Track Time with the Stopwatch

- Click the **Stopwatch** tab, and swipe the stopwatch to switch between analog and digital faces.

- Tap **Start,** and the timing will continue to count even if you launch a different app.

- Tap **Lap** to record a split or lap.

- Tap the **Stop** button to record the final time.

- Tap the **Reset** to clear the stopwatch.

Chapter 29: The Translate App

Translate text and voice from one language to another. You may also choose to download some languages to use when your device is not connected to a network.

Translate Text or Voice

- Open the Translate app, put your iPhone to portrait orientation, and then press the **Translate** tab at the bottom.

- You will see two languages at the top of your screen. The first option is to choose the original language of whatever you want to translate, while the second language is for the new language.

- Tap 🎤 to speak and say a phrase or click the '**Enter Text**' field, type in a phrase, and click **Go.**

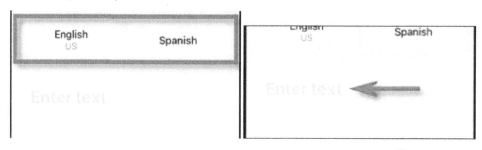

- The translation will come up on your screen – tap ▶ to replay audio translation, tap ☆ to add the translation to the Favorites tab, or tap 📖 to look up the meaning of the word in the dictionary.

Translate a Conversation

While in conversation mode, your screen is split into two to show the translated and transcribed text from the two speakers, followed by the audio translation. You can also use this mode for downloaded languages without an active internet connection.

- Open the Translate app, put your iPhone to portrait orientation, and then press the **Translate** tab at the bottom.

- Tap  and then take turns to speak and view the translated words.

English (US)

Where is the train station

Spanish

¿Dónde está la estación de tren?

Translate with Large Text

Increase the size of the text on the translation screen.

- Put your iPhone to portrait orientation, press the **Translate** tab, and then tap .

Download Languages for Offline Translation

To download languages on the Translate app:

- Click the Translate tab at the bottom, then click one of the language tabs at the top of the screen.
- Swipe down on your screen to the **'Available Offline Languages'** option, tap a language you want, and then press **Done.**

Chapter 30: The Reminders App

Keep track of all your to-do lists, use the app for tasks around the house, create a shopping list, and more. A new feature called the smart list helps to organize your lists and reminders automatically.

Create a New Reminder

- Open the Reminder app, click on **New Reminder** and then type in what you want to be reminded of.

- Click and choose a date and time for the action.

- Click on the icon to assign the reminder to someone in your contact.

- Tap the icon to add a location to the reminder.

- Click on the icon to add a photo or scanned document to the reminder.

- Click on the icon to set a flag for the reminder.

- Tap the icon, and type in more details about the reminder in the **Notes** field.

- Enter a web address in the URL field.

- Turn on the '**When Messaging**' switch to get a reminder whenever you chat with a selected contact.

- Click **Priority** to set a priority for the reminder.

- Tap **Done** to save.

Mark a Reminder as Complete

- Scroll to the reminder you want to complete, and you will find an empty circle beside it. Tap the circle to complete the action. You will no longer see the reminder in the list.

- To see your completed reminders, press and select the **'Show Completed'** option.

Edit Multiple Reminders

- Open the Reminders app, tap , press **Reminders,** and tap all the ones you wish to edit.

- Scroll to the bottom of the screen and click the action you want to apply to the selected reminders.

Move Reminders to a New List

- Press the reminder, press the icon, click on **List,** and tap a different list.

Create a Subtask

You can create a subtask under a reminder that you can complete even before completing the parent task.

- Swipe right on the desired reminder, and click on **Indent.**

- Alternatively, drag one reminder and drop it on top of another reminder.

Note that deleting, completing, or moving the parent task will automatically delete, complete or move the subtasks.

Reorder or Delete Reminders

- Press the reminder you wish to move, then drag it to a different position.
- To delete the reminder, swipe left on it and tap **Delete.**
- Tap your screen twice with your three fingers to quickly undo the action.

Change Reminders Settings

- Tap **Reminders** in the Settings app and click on **Accounts** to add accounts like Yahoo, Gmail, iCloud, and more.
- Tap **Today Notification** to choose the default time for receiving notifications for reminders you didn't input a specific time.
- Tap **Default List** to choose a default list for any new reminders not created inside a specific list.
- Tap **Mute Notifications** to stop receiving notifications for the reminders.
- Tap **Show as Overdue** to have your overdue all-day reminder turn red on the scheduled date.

Create Lists

Create a list and add similar reminders to the same list. E.g., a shopping list.

- Open **Reminders** and click the **'Add List'** option at the bottom of your screen.
- Give your list a name, choose a color and a symbol for easy identification.

- To edit the list at any time, swipe left on the list, press ⓘ and make your changes.

- To reorder and move the list, press firmly on the list and move it to a different location/ group.

- To delete the list and all its content, swipe left on it and tap 🗑

Create a Group

After creating lists for your reminders, you can then create groups to contain the different categories of lists. For example, a group that contains all the celebration reminders like birthdays, anniversaries, etc.

- Open Reminders and tap **Edit** at the top right.

- Tap the '**Add Group'** option, give your group a name, and tap **Create.**

- A quicker way to create a group is to drag one list and drop it on top of another list.

- To edit the group at any time, swipe left on it, press ⓘ and make your changes.

- To delete the group and all its content, swipe left and tap 🗑 .

Use Smart Lists

Smart Lists helps you to track and organize your reminders automatically.

- Open **Reminders** and tap the **Today** option to view your activities for today as well as your overdue reminders.

- Tap the **'Assigned to Me'** option to view the reminders assigned to you.

- Tap the **'Scheduled'** option to display the reminders by time or date.

- Tap the **'All'** section to show all the reminders you created.

Share a List

You can only share a list with people using iCloud. Whoever has access to the list can edit and mark the reminders as completed.

- Click on a list, press ⬭ and click the **'Share List'** option.

- Select a method to send the invitation.

Assign Reminders in a Shared List

After you share a list, you can assign different reminders in the list to different people.

- Open a reminder in a list, tap 👤 and choose someone from the shared list.

Chapter 31: The App Store

Read featured stories, find new apps, and enjoy new tricks and tips for your iPhone.

Find and Download Apps

- Open the iOS app store on your phone.
- Click the **Today** tab at the bottom to see the featured apps & stories.
- Click the **Apps** tab to browse by category, see the top charts, or see the newly released apps.
- Click the **Search** tab to search for apps and games.
- Click on an app to see details like file size, privacy information, reviews, ratings, etc.
- Then click $\quad$ GET $\quad$ to download the app if it is a free app, or press the price to download paid apps. Any app you previously purchased will have the ☁ icon instead of the price – and you can always re-download the app at no extra cost.
- Authenticate your action with your passcode or Face ID to finish.

Share an App

- Click on an app in the app store, press ⬆ and click on **Gift App,** or select a sharing option for others.

Redeem or Send Gift Card

To gift or redeem a gift card from iTunes or the app store,

- Touch your profile image at the top right side of the app store.
- Then select an option:

> ➢ **Send Gift Card by Email**

> ➢ **Redeem Gift Card or Code**

Use App Clips

With the App Clip, you no longer need to install an app to enjoy some services on the app. You can use the App Clips to order food, pay for parking, and more in Maps, Messages, Safari, or even in the real world. You can open an App Clip in different ways:

- Click the App Clip link in the app.
- Scan the QR code displayed at physical locations like payment terminals or restaurants.
- Position your device near the NFC (near-field communications) tag.

You will find the App Clip close to the bottom of your screen.

- For some App Clips, click the banner at the upper part of the screen to open the full app in the Apple App Store.

Find Recently Used App Clips

To see all the App Clips you used in the past,

- Go to the **App Library** and tap the '**Recently Added**' option.

Remove App Clips

App Clips you use are saved on your iPhone. To remove them,

- Tap **App Clips** in the Settings app and then tap the '**Remove All App Clips**' option.

Subscribe to Apple Arcade

Apple Arcade is Apple's gaming subscription service that gives users unlimited access to a collection of games.

- Click the **Arcade** tab in the App Store.
- Then tap **Subscribe** to begin a monthly subscription or tap **Try it Free** for a free one-month subscription.
- Confirm your purchase with your Apple ID or Face ID.

Cancel Apple Arcade Subscription

- Touch your profile image at the top right side of the app store.
- Press **Subscriptions,** click **Apple Arcade** & select **Cancel Subscription.**

Manage Your Subscriptions

- Touch your profile image at the top right side of the app store.
- Press **Subscriptions** to see all your active subscriptions and make any changes.

Change App Store Settings

- Tap **App Store** in the Settings app, scroll to **Automatic Downloads,** and turn on the **'Apps'** switch if you want the iPhone to automatically download the apps you purchased on your other Apple devices.

- Turn on the **'App Updates'** switch to automatically update your apps.

- Turn on the **'Offload Unused Apps'** switch to instruct the iPhone to automatically remove any apps you didn't use in a while.

- Turn on the **'Video Autoplay'** switch to permit the iPhone to automatically play app preview videos when you scroll to an app.

- To control how the iPhone uses your cellular data for download, move to **Cellular Data,** and turn on the **'Automatic Downloads'** switch to allow the iPhone to download apps using your cellular data.

- Click on **App Download t**o choose options for downloading apps above 200MB.

Chapter 32: 'Sign in with Apple' on the iPhone 12

Sign in with Apple is a more private, safe, and easy way to sign in to websites and third-party apps using your Apple ID. You won't need to create new details for such websites, and your account will have two-factor authentication. You can only use this service with participating websites and apps with the 'Sign in with Apple' button – no need filling out forms, using your social media account, or setting up a new password.

These participating websites and apps will only ask for your name and email address to create your account.

Set up an Account to Sign in with Apple

To create an account with a participating website or app,

- Tap the **'Sign in with Apple'** option and then continue with the directions onscreen.

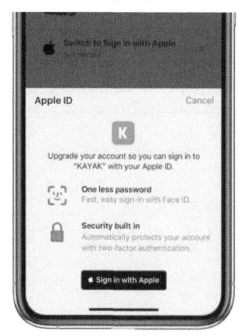

- Some websites and apps may not request your email address and name. You will only need to authenticate with your Face ID for such sites and apps before you start using the app.

- If the app or website requests for your name and email address, Apple will show the name and email address on your Apple ID account – tap the name to edit it.

- Click the **Share My Email** option to use your personal email address on the site or tap the **'Hide My Email'** option if you do not want to use your personal email address.

- If you choose the **'Hide my Email'** option, Apple will create a random email address for you, and all emails received sent to the random email address from the websites or app will be forwarded to your personal email address.

- After selecting an email option, click **Continue**, authenticate your access, and then begin to use the app.

Sign in to your Account

After using the Sign in with Apple option to create an account with a participating website or app, you won't need to sign in to the app again on your device. However, if prompted to sign in,

- Tap the **'Sign in with Apple'** option, and tap **Continue.**

- Then approve your sign in with your Face ID.

Change the Address Used for Receiving forwarded Emails

If you choose the 'Hide my Email' option and have more than one email address linked with your Apple ID, you can choose your preferred email address for receiving the forwarded email.

- Tap your name in the **Settings** app, tap **Name, Phone Numbers, Email,** and then click on **Forward To.**

- Select the email address you want and tap **Done.**

Change your Sign in with Apple Settings

Change the Sign in with Apple settings you use on a website or app

- Tap your name in the **Settings** app, and tap **Password and Security.**

- Click the **'Using Your Apple ID'** option and select an app.

- Turn off the **'Forward To'** switch to stop receiving emails from that app.

- Tap the **Stop Using Apple ID** option to stop using Sign in with Apple on that site or app. You may need to create another account when next you want to sign in with the app.

Chapter 33: Weather App

Get weather reports for your current location or any other location in the world. Apple also sends alerts about severe weather conditions as well as notifications on if snow or rain is on the way.

To get a forecast for your present location, you need to turn on Location Services:

- Tap **Privacy** in the Settings app, then turn on the **'Location Services'** option.

Check Weather Conditions and Forecast

Only users in the U.S. can receive Next-Hour Precipitation.

- Open the Weather app and swipe the hourly display to view the hourly forecast.

- View the current local weather conditions on the home page.

- Swipe down to see wind speed, humidity, air quality, and more.

- Scroll to the top of the screen to view alerts about severe weather conditions like flash floods and winter storms.

- Scroll to view next-hour precipitation, that is when snow or rain is coming in the next hour.

- Swipe right or left on the screen or tap ⋮≡ to view weather in a different location.

Add or Delete Locations in the Weather App

Add locations that you want to receive weather conditions for.

- Open the Weather app and tap ⋮≡ to view your weather list.

- To search and add a new location, tap the $\mathcal{Q}$ icon, input an airport code, zip code, or city to view the weather, then click **Add.**

- If you do not want a location on your list, swipe left on it and tap **Delete.**

- To reorder the locations on the list, press down on a location and then change its position.

Switch Between Celsius and Fahrenheit

- Tap ☰ in the Weather app and choose either °C or °F at the bottom of the list.

Index

Made in the USA
Monee, IL
10 January 2021